SCIENCE IN
THE PRIMARY
SCHOOL

YVONNE GARSON

The Author

Yvonne Garson is Lecturer in Education at the University of
Keele. She has taught in primary schools in England and in the
USA, and she has taught science at secondary level. She is co-
author of *Schooling in the Middle Years* (Trentham Books,
1982).

Subjects in the Primary School
Series editor: Professor John Eggleston

SCIENCE IN THE PRIMARY SCHOOL

YVONNE GARSON

ROUTLEDGE

LONDON

First published in 1988 by
Routledge
11 New Fetter Lane, London EC4P 4EE

Set in Sabon 10/11pt.
by Columns of Reading
and printed in Great Britain
by Cox & Wyman Ltd
Reading, Berks

British Library Cataloguing-in-Publication Data
Garson, Yvonne
  Science in the primary school.—
  (Subjects in the primary school).
  1. Science——Study and teaching
  (Elementary)——Great Britain
  I. Title II. Series
  372.3'5'0941   LB1585.5.G7

ISBN 0-415-00224-9

Contents

Acknowledgments

Thanks are due to Dave Walley and his colleagues at Burton Primary School, to Dave Perry and his colleagues at Florence Primary School, and to Jo Horrobin and all my other colleagues who have given so freely of their thoughts and ideas.

I am also grateful to the following for permission to reproduce from their material: Macdonald Educational for the workcard on p. 3, and for the flow chart from *Holes, Gaps and Cavities* on p. 10, Longman for the workcards on pp. 4, 19 and 22, and for the extract on p. 61; and Cheshire County Council for the flow chart on p. 66.

Series Editor's Preface

After a decade of declining rolls, the number of children in primary schools is once again rising in most countries in the western world. The rise brings in its train an urgent demand for new teachers and ministries, school authorities and training institutions are turning to university graduates, offering one-year or other shortened courses rather than the conventional three- or four-year training course.

Such students know that they are keenly sought. Not only does the shortened course make them more immediately available to the schools, but also their expertise is highly appropriate to the widespread demand for real subject specialism to be available in the primary school curriculum.

But the translation of degree-level study into effective primary teaching is a difficult task – particularly in the short postgraduate course. This series is designed to help students to make the transition more readily. Each volume helps the reader to see the similarities between study at school and university and goes on, with advice, example and explanation, to show how subject knowledge can be structured and presented effectively in a primary school curriculum. Above all, the series aims to help beginning graduate teachers to transmit the enthusiasm that has led them to become specialists to new generations of young people.

John Eggleston

1

Primary science in perspective

This is a book for teachers and would-be teachers whose tolerance for rhetoric and fine words has reached a low ebb. For those teachers who are feeling pressurised to provide 'effective primary science' and are looking for models to work from, clues to success or examples of good practice, this book attempts to set a framework within which they can encourage their pupils to explore, invent, discover and learn scientific skills while they themselves realistically monitor the children's progress. This framework needs to be contextualised, so this introductory chapter is devoted to providing a backcloth to possible teaching strategies by examining current thinking as well as taking a brief look at the contributions made during the last twenty years of curriculum development.

Ask teachers, pupils, parents or educational administrators to think of words that express the feelings evoked by their classroom experiences of science and you will come up with a list not dissimilar to the one provided here:

fun	repetitive
difficult	old-fashioned
time-consuming	confusing
what if?	wonderful
exciting	not relevant
messy	practical
great	investigating
too much like maths	finding out
absorbing	incomprehensible
boring	challenging
relevant to everyday life	frustrating
thought-provoking	

Some words occur more frequently than others and the range of emotions expressed is surprising, but one of the most noteworthy things is that few people have no reactions at all – talking to people about their memories, perceptions and experiences associated with science usually produces a strong emotional response. A variety of people, all connected in some way with primary schools, produced the above list of words and phrases associated with science; in a simple way it highlights the wide divergence of views held by those concerned with organising and implementing primary science programmes as to what science actually entails. Any primary science curriculum must be sensitive to this diversity, for if it is not it will fail to capitalise on the existing skills and expertise of classroom teachers, and undermine their confidence in science teaching. Thus, science in the primary school must reflect a flexibility of approach; in this way all the variety of experience and differences in training of primary teachers can be seen as valuable assets – pupils don't all have to do science in the same way.

The emphasis and direction of science teaching in primary schools have altered in recent years, with perhaps the most radical change being its inclusion in the primary curriculum at all. That is not to say that science has been excluded in the past but rather that it has depended upon the choice of individual teachers – by contrast with mathematics and language teaching. If science is to be part of every primary pupil's experience some schools and teachers are going to have to make changes in their classroom activities. However, before it is accepted that change is necessary, it is important not only to examine what is meant by science and what bearing this has on the education of 5 – 11-year-old children, but also to look critically at the supposed differences between science teaching today and that which was practised twenty years ago.

At its very best, what are the essential qualities of primary science? It is my view that it should be seen not as a subject to be done at set times in rooms with specialist facilities but rather as a series of explorations and a way of solving problems which can be applied anywhere, adapting whatever materials happen to be at hand. This is in contrast to the situation in which pupils become dependent on a supply of traditional scientific equipment before they can work in a scientific way, for if this is

You will need

A sausage balloon
A straw
Adhesive tape
Nylon line

What to do

Cut two 5cm lengths of straw.

1 Slide the two lengths of straw on to the nylon line.

2 Fix the nylon line tightly across the room. It must not sag.

3 Have two pieces of adhesive tape ready for use.

4 Blow up the balloon. Ask your partner to stick the tape to the balloon as shown in the picture.

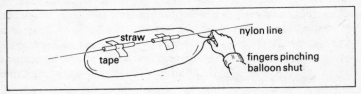

5 Take the balloon to the end of the line and let it go.

Figure 1.1 An example of a workcard giving specific instructions (Source: 'Propulsion', Section 3, *Flying Starts Here, Science Horizons*, Level 26)

the case the discoveries they can make and the areas in which they can solve problems are likely to be severely restricted.

Obviously it is important to establish in principle what doing primary science actually entails. Science for primary-aged pupils must be an active and not a passive process. Passivity here is not merely synonymous with a lack of experimentation (indeed, it can include doing experiments, especially if these are carried out in a mechanical – and mechanistic – way) but can also involve, for example, following the instructions on a worksheet much like the recipe in a cook book. Figure 1.1 gives an example of just such a worksheet.

Another example of this passivity is found when a teacher instructs a pupil to carry out certain procedures. Either the verbal instructions to the children telling them how to fold a filter paper or the diagrammatic instructions shown in Figure 1.2 illustrate this.

For in such cases, although the pupils may be doing things,

3

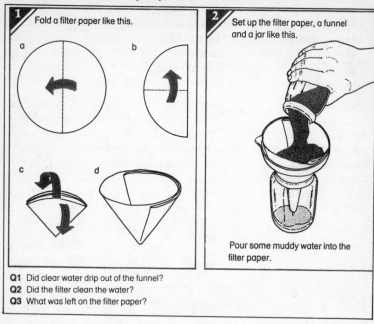

1 Fold a filter paper like this.

a

b

c

d

2 Set up the filter paper, a funnel and a jar like this.

Pour some muddy water into the filter paper.

Q1 Did clear water drip out of the funnel?
Q2 Did the filter clean the water?
Q3 What was left on the filter paper?

Figure 1.2 Diagrams showing how to fold a filter paper
(Source: 'Making things pure', card 29A, *Look: Primary Science*)

there is little opportunity for them to develop the intellectual skills of true problem-solving.

Furthermore, 'activity' in this context is liable to misinterpretation, for it can entail processes other than doing experiments, although these are clearly the most important element in doing science. Some excellent 'scientific investigations' can be found in the ASE publication *Primary Science*, spring 1986, written up by Cynthia Lawson, the teacher with responsibility for science. Here the pupils from Frodsham CE Controlled Primary School in Cheshire looked at a local industry; this is illustrated in Figure 1.3.

Other aspects that come under the umbrella of this investigation might include pupils searching for solutions to questions that are outside their immediate experience by using reference material to increase the scope of their knowledge and understanding of a particular topic. The topic used by that school included some research using old documents.

Class 5 studied the distribution of salt beds and the problem of subsidence. Interested by the Museum, they found out about the history of the mines, and read an 1866 report about the employment of children in the works – and were pleased to know they were not sent underground.

Also, curiosity aroused by investigations can lead pupils outside their own classrooms. The realisation that the science that they are doing has applications in their own lives is an important part of their scientific education. Figure 1.4 shows how pupils used a local doctor as a resource and documents their communications with a local food manufacturer.

Some of these activities may be more effective and successful than others in enabling pupils to understand the nature of science, and, given this, teachers need to select work suitable for their particular pupils. However, it must also be remembered that flexibility of approach and a range of varied activities are beneficial and it may not always be possible to choose the very best. It is essential that we do not forget that there are many ways of arriving at the goals of good primary science. This is an important point to bear in mind when considering the details of curriculum planning.

Evidence from data collected by the APU in *Science Report for Teachers: Science at Age 11*[1] gives some indication of the existing strengths within primary schools and points to some weaknesses which could be taken into account in curriculum planning. The survey suggests that 'schools are providing suitable opportunities for the children to develop general skills such as observing, measuring and keeping written records which are widely applicable across the curriculum'. All these are skills which any primary teacher would claim to foster during their classroom activities – mathematics, language development and topic or project work. For the development of primary science, however, they are not deemed to be enough, and alone they do not provide a sound enough basis for the discovery and problem-solving activities which are central to scientific enquiry. For these the APU report goes on to suggest that other skills are required:

> Given this sound base, there is now a need to consider how to help children acquire these more specific science skills such as:

Frodsham is in a salt mining area and is surrounded by large chemical plants. Most of the school's parents are employed in those industries, and they were as enthusiastic as the children when we chose SALT for a school project.

With a grant from the Society of Chemical Industries we were able to buy equipment which made our experiments easier, such as two simple digital balances, a selection of thermometers, and more measuring cylinders and funnels. All five classes in the school took part. Some ideas were taken up at different levels by several classes, others by only one. To start the project we all visited the Lion Salt Works. Younger children also went to the seashore, and older ones to the Salt Museum.

Does salt really preserve food?

Class 2 knew that some people thought so.

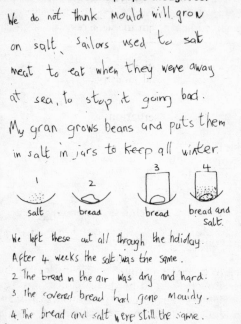

We do not think mould will grow on salt. Sailors used to salt meat to eat when they were away at sea, to stop it going bad.
My gran grows beans and puts them in salt in jars to keep all winter.

1 salt
2 bread
3 bread
4 bread and salt

We left these out all through the holiday.
After 4 weeks the salt was the same.
2 The bread in the air was dry and hard.
3 The covered bread had gone mouldy.
4. The bread and salt were still the same.

Would more salt dissolve in hot water?

Robin explains how **Class 2** found out.

"We have put 80 ml of water in a beaker. We have put 7g of salt into the water. We have stirred it. Some salt is in the bottom and no more will dissolve. We heated the water and the salt at the bottom dissolved. Then we put in 2g more and they dissolved.

More salt dissolves in hot water than cold. The spoon seemed to be bigger in the water."

Class 4 ran into difficulties when several children did a similar experiment. They agreed about the number of spoonsful of salt which dissolved in 250 ml of cold water, but had several answers for the hot water. Why? After some discussion they decided that some had used warm water and others very hot water. When they all used the same temperature they got the same results.

Figure 1.3 Science investigations into salt
(Source: 'Starting from a local industry', *Primary Science*, 19, spring 1986)

defining patterns in observations
giving explanations
predicting
hypothesising
controlling variables and
planning investigations

in which children are much less competent.

A consideration of each of these will feature in subsequent chapters.

One thing to be borne in mind by any primary school teacher who may feel overwhelmed by these 'failings' in their pupils is that these skills were also found to be lacking in many thirteen- and fifteen-year-olds. However, the primary sector provides a much greater cause for optimism about shifting the direction and emphasis of science teaching in the future because of the greater relative autonomy of the primary school teacher and the lack of constraints imposed by external examinations.

In order to understand why so much government money (mainly in the form of education support grants and extra in-service provision) has been provided in the 1980s for the development of science curricula, it is necessary to trace the fortunes of science within the primary curriculum in the preceding two decades. Why has science in the primary school become such a contentious issue? This backward glance does provide some explanations.

The late 1960s – the post-Plowden Report era – heralded a growth of optimism in curriculum planning, backed up by a buoyant economy. There was talk of pupils finding out for themselves. The questions that were asked in the Plowden Report[2] are indicative of the sort of primary teaching that was being openly endorsed.

> Has *finding out* proved to be better than *being told*? Have methods been worked out through which discovery can be stimulated and guided, and children develop from it a coherent body of knowledge?
>
> Do children learn more through active co-operation or by passive obedience?

The report not only asked questions; in seeking answers to those (and other questions) it stated that: 'We draw attention to the best practices we have found as a pointer to the direction in which all schools should move.' And these best practices openly encouraged the class teacher to explore with her pupils, to act as a guide and consultant, to become a manager of learning rather than a purveyor of facts. That indeed was the popular rhetoric at the time – even though, as we now know, twenty years later, the reality bore little resemblance to these words. The majority of the nation's primary schools did not substantially change into the free and easy child-centred establishments that popular myth would have had us believe. It was in this climate that *Science 5/13*[3] and *Nuffield Primary Science*[4] were spawned. Both are series of resource books for teachers full of excellent ideas for the kind of active discovery work that fitted the Plowden recommendations. It is also worth noting here that

Do we need salt?

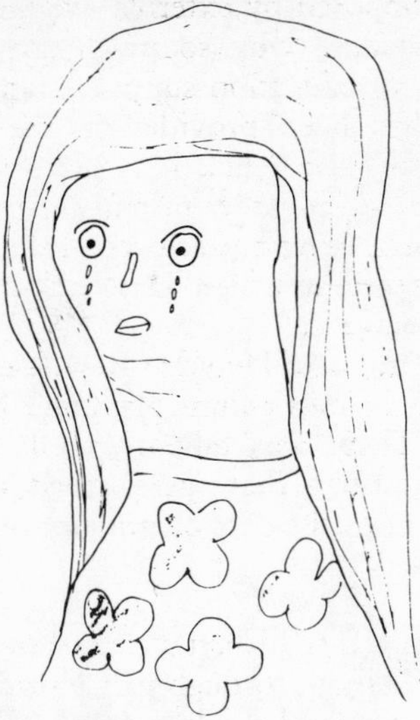

Penny
Class 3   When we cry we lose salt through our tears.

A parent who is a doctor came to talk to us. He explained that our bodies needed some salt to work properly, but too much was not good for us.

Afterwards **Class 2** children found that there was salt in many popular foods from baked beans to Kit Kat. They wrote to several manufacturers to ask why they included salt in their products. Most replied that they used very little, mainly to enhance flavours.

We made bread with and without salt. We all liked it better with salt.

Figure 1.4   An example of students extending their work beyond the classroom
(Source: 'Starting from a local industry')

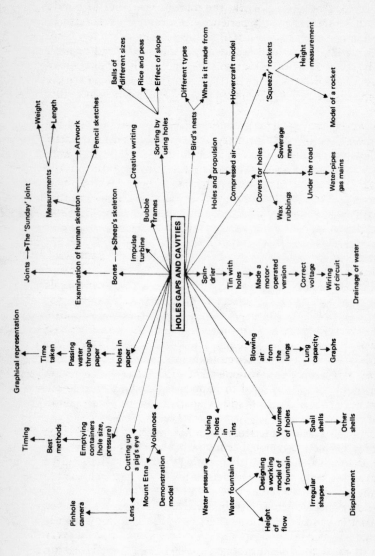

Figure 1.5 Flow chart illustrating some possibilities for science topics
(Source: *Holes, Gaps and Cavities, Science 5/13*)

science was seen to find its place in the primary curriculum as part of topic or project work, the topics arising out of pupils' immediate interests and experience. An example of this can be found in one of the *Science 5/13* Teachers' Guides, *Holes, Gaps and Cavities*. Many of those ideas are developed into possible pupils' practical work in that volume, and the flow chart shown in Figure 1.5 illustrates the sort of association between science and the rest of the curriculum that was being advocated at that time.

However, the instigators of the projects underestimated the traditionalism of most primary schools. This mistake partly explains why many of the sets of *Science 5/13* books that were bought for staffroom use remained collecting dust on the shelves. The investigative, exploratory approach that was suggested in those schemes was assumed to be similar to that which was already going on in classrooms – after all, that was what the media and the education world were giving people to believe was the new progressive education. But this was far from the reality. The majority of teachers were using traditional, didactic methods of teaching for all areas of the curriculum and the majority had no science activities planned for their pupils beyond a collection of objects on a nature table. It is not surprising, then, that teachers found it difficult to incorporate this new science into their normal classroom practice. The science material was extremely innovative, and what few people realised was that the rethinking that would be necessary on the part of teachers to implement such changes in teaching style could not be expected to happen so suddenly nor be led from what was then (and still is now) a minority curriculum area.

So, in all ways, the science initiatives, whether Nuffield or Schools Council originated, contained changes that were too radical for the educational climate of their time. The kind of innovations required of teachers were at that time isolated within science.

Despite backlashes against this supposed progressivism in the 1970s the position of primary science did not substantially change – it was still not established as an essential part of every primary-aged child's education. Publishers and authors, aware that the attempts at persuading teachers to use resource materials as a guide to their preparation of work had not been very successful, produced worksheet schemes for the pupils to use. One reason given for this was that the hard-pressed primary teacher could have well tested and tried experiments that really worked for their pupils to do; they would also eliminate any insecurity felt by the teacher who might be unused to handling open-ended investigations. Science, where it existed, once again returned to fit in with the mainstream of activities: pupils might indeed by physically doing things with their hands but in fact, in the main, they were carefully following instructions – engaged in 'passive' science.

The HMI survey of primary schools,[5] carried out eleven years after the publication of the Plowden Report, highlights just how much the mood and rhetoric had changed in that short space of time. Compare these extracts from the HMI Report with those quoted in previous pages.

> Curriculum content should be selected not only to suit the interests and abilities of the children and to provide for the progressive development of the basic skills, but because it is important in its own right... . The teachers' need for a thorough knowledge of the subject becomes more marked as the children get older.

The teacher who may well have been inhibited by the open-ended approach could now feel equally threatened by the suggestion that a certain body of knowledge is required before successful science teaching can take place.

The debate concerning which scheme is the better, more appropriate, most suited to a particular age range or the most lavishly produced can be a lengthy one and avoids the central issue. As has been previously noted, if pupils are only following instructions, they are not as likely to be predicting, hypothesising, controlling variables or planning investigations which are, as claimed by the APU in their survey, to be the 'more specific scientific skills'. Previous initiatives have clearly not succeeded in establishing science in primary schools. Small groups of enthusiasts have shown what value can be gained by teaching science to young children, but this is as the result of individuals, not education authorities, or as a result of government pressure. Teachers themselves are the key to successful science:

those of us that are involved in initial training, in-service provision or curriculum development must not only show the value of including science in the list of acceptable primary school activities but must also come to terms with the very varied biographies of the teachers who will be involved with those pupils. Science education at secondary level, despite changes in emphasis brought about by the Nuffield Science syllabuses, has not until now fostered an enquiring, experimental or hypothesising approach to learning. Some of the blame for this lies in the external examination structure which constrains teachers and pupils in secondary schools. Experimental work in secondary schools is often turgid and boring and can be a long way from the dynamic, open-ended explorations that curriculum planners have been advocating; that sort of prescriptive science is probably the only experience that most primary school teachers had when they themselves were pupils. Women predominate in the teaching force in primary schools, and we have evidence to show that few girls pursue the physical sciences or technology beyond third-form level. Biology is their only science in many instances and, regrettably, that particular science is taught in a very unexperimental way in secondary schools. It can be taught as a descriptive subject – a good memory and neat handwriting can count for a lot.

In reality, the majority of primary school teachers have never experienced the joy of experimenting, finding out by predicting, hypothesising, controlling variables or planning investigations. They may never have felt the excitement of discovery, so it is really not surprising that many teachers cannot engender in their pupils something they have never felt themselves. Nor is it surprising that anyone should feel insecure with a way of working that is outside their own experience.

One thing stands out clearly in the 1980s, and that is that the pressure is on schools, headteachers and every classroom teacher to:

> include the teaching of science among the curricular aims which it formally adopts...develop programmes of work... monitor its own progress.[6]

This policy statement continues to be prescriptive when it adds:

All class teachers, without exception, should include at least some science in their teaching.

and that:

The school needs to have at its disposal at least one teacher with the capacity, knowledge and insight to make science education for primary pupils a reality.

and further that these teachers' roles are defined within the school as:

Science consultants or experts [who are expected to]...stimulate science teaching throughout the school and provide help and support for their colleagues.

A specifically prescriptive paper has emerged from the DES and the expectations are clearly spelt out in terms of teachers' various roles, be they as initiator or implementer. The problems for those people involved in initial or in-service training is not a new one: there is a reluctance on the part of teachers to include science in primary school pupils' activities and a way has to be found not only to make it possible but also to make it a pleasurable experience for all involved.

How can this be achieved now when efforts throughout the last twenty years have not proved immensely successful? This question raises such complex issues that it could perhaps engender a publication in its own right! Two factors do emerge in the debate as having particular significance. The first is that a directive has been given – the DES *Statement of Policy* gives explicit instructions for school practice – and this has clearly created impetus for change. Science is beginning to be seen as an essential and desirable activity for the under 11-year-olds, and headteachers are being persuaded of the need for its inclusion in the curriculum. Furthermore, money is now being invested in support and in-service training for teachers and not in large-scale national projects which produce written materials for either teacher or pupils. For some of the reasons already outlined, teachers lack confidence, so local education authorities are investing money in advisory teachers: teams of good, experienced practitioners to work alongside classroom teachers, helping them to interpret published resources and supporting them through difficult periods of change and adjustments in their own teaching styles. It is easier to have a go at something new if you have the help and support of a sympathetic colleague who has tried it out before you.

There is a very real danger in this rush to put science on the map in each primary school. Unless teachers are given the help and support of carefully planned in-service programmes they may buy and use commercially produced packages of workcards which may keep pupils busy but do not extend those skills we have been extolling. We are asking teachers to become confident enough to say, 'I don't know the answers', allow their pupils to make mistakes, and learn new things alongside their pupils. This is where a carefully planned and organised framework within which experimentation can take place can provide sufficient security to enable teachers as well as pupils to experience the joy of discovery. Primary school pupils are curious, and interested in their environment. Scientific investigations merely enable them to extend and build on what is already there. The problems of implementing primary science programmes in schools are not new ones; having set the scene and explained briefly why these problems have occurred, it has become clear that any solutions do not lie in the production of new resources but rather in the judicious selection of already published materials that can be used in a different way. What is now happening in schools around the country seems to indicate that local authorities are taking heed of past failures – individual teachers have become the focus of in-service training initiatives and science *is* being taught in some primary schools throughout the country. This provides us not only with an opportunity to use and adapt materials from the wealth of resources available but also to take examples from existing good practice. That is what this book sets out to do.

2

The framework for planning science activities

What is science? This question can be answered from a variety of viewpoints. 'What is science?' an article in the book *Approaching Primary Science*,[1] gives a concise and useful introduction to the practical aspects covered in this chapter. Here we are concerned with establishing a framework, an organisational structure, so that effective science learning can take place. Before this can occur, it is necessary to have some clear notion about what schools should be aiming for.

> ...if children are to learn Science...we must give them respect for observations rather than the pronouncements of the textbook and teacher prophets. ...we must see to it that children understand experimentation as a means of compelling nature to answer their questions. ...children must know that *no one really knows*. If we can give children these insights, they will have learnt science, no matter what content they have covered.

That small extract voices the sentiments and philosophy behind the following chapters, which are anecdotal and full of advice and ideas for teachers seeking help in teaching primary science. What is described in Figure 2.1 is a suggested sequence of activities, starting with the heading 'Ask a question', that teachers can use as a base or framework for their planning. Given as a subheading under each actual activity is a list of skills that should be developed at this stage. Although these may appear at first glance to be activities arranged in a linear sequence, in practice, a cycle would be a more realistic description: pupils are encouraged to return to certain activities

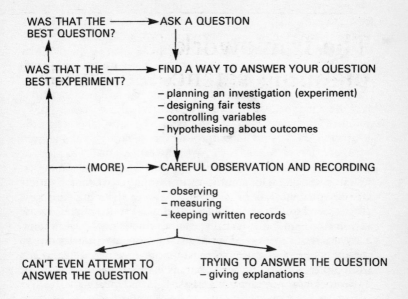

Figure 2.1 A suggested sequence of activities that will provide a framework for planning scientific investigations

to verify, collect more information or maybe simply to find out more about something. The essence of successful primary science is encouraging and teaching pupils to ask the kinds of questions that will lead to investigations. These must be questions that they are genuinely interested in and that it is possible for them to answer within their own field of ability and experience. Children must learn to ask 'what' and 'how' questions, not 'why' questions. The first two can usually be answered through experimentation and observation, but 'why' questions can lead us into consideration of the mystical and metaphysical. Young children can sort out '*what* happens when different balls are dropped onto the floor' and they can even sort out *how* to find out whether dropping them on different surfaces makes a difference. But an answer to the question '*Why* do balls bounce?' is beyond the realm of the junior scientist!

Once the question has been formulated (how this can be encouraged to happen is something that I shall return to later), teacher and pupils will have to work together to plan investigations. This second stage in the sequence, 'Find a way to answer your question', is what inexperienced teachers will find most threatening, and it is where the temptation to rely solely on workcards and worksheets giving pupils instructions will be the greatest. There are uses for these commercially produced schemes, but at this stage of a pupil's scientific education there is no substitute for the mental vigour required of them by planning their own investigations. The list of processes given as subheadings at this stage – planning an investigation, designing fair tests, controlling variables, hypothesising – should not be dismissed as overwhelming: this is a comprehensive list of possibilities, an ideal to keep at the back of one's mind. Realistically, some pupils will find some activities less easy to cope with; they may need to work on very specific skills, and this is one situation in which a workcard from *Look – Primary Science*[2] may be used selectively to an individual pupil's great advantage. I am advocating here that particular activities giving pupils extra opportunity to practise skills could be used in addition to their scientific, investigative work, as and when they are needed. In the simple example given, two variables are introduced into the problem of efficiently dissolving sugar – temperature of the water, and size of sugar lumps. The work card shown in Figure 2.2 gives pupils exact instructions and does not attempt to encourage pupils to plan or design their own experiments. However, if individuals are having trouble with understanding the importance of constants and variables these instructions can be of enormous value as they provide help with learning and practising specific skills.

The introduction of variables can also often occur through disagreements from within a group of children. They often want to investigate different aspects of the same problem. A group of 7- and 8-year-olds were arguing vociferously in a corner and when their teacher intervened, she found that they only needed her assistance in determining how Mark could test his theory that only light things float. Mary said some floated because they were flat and Andy claimed that only wood floated anyway. They introduced three variables, weight, shape

What makes sugar dissolve faster?

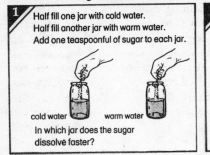

1 Half fill one jar with cold water.
Half fill another jar with warm water.
Add one teaspoonful of sugar to each jar.

cold water   warm water

In which jar does the sugar
dissolve faster?

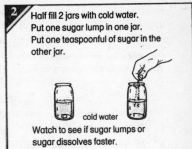

2 Half fill 2 jars with cold water.
Put one sugar lump in one jar.
Put one teaspoonful of sugar in the
other jar.

cold water

Watch to see if sugar lumps or
sugar dissolves faster.

Q3 Does sugar dissolve faster in warm water or cold water?
Q4 Which dissolves faster – sugar or sugar lumps?

Figure 2.2 Instructions such as these control the constants and variables
(Source: 'Dissolving things', card 27A, *Look: Primary Science*)

and material, and with negotiation, persuasion and the provision of some information and materials the teacher helped those children progress further down the 'scientific sequence'. The teacher's notes in Figure 2.3 show some of the discussion and negotiations that took place between teacher and pupils.

'Designing fair tests' is the aspect of science teaching that teachers need to worry about least. As long as the pupils are involved in the planning of their experiments and are making some of the decisions themselves concerning setting up the activities it is hard to exclude fair testing – a child's sense of justice will ensure that. How often have you heard a child complain 'that's not fair'?

Under the heading 'Careful observation and recording,' observing, measuring and record-keeping are skills that pupils are encouraged to acquire in many different ways in the infant and junior classes. That does not mean that children may know what to measure or how to record in the most useful way for the particular task they are engaged in. Surprisingly, even in junior schools where subjects are not very clearly delineated, children will complain that they are having to 'do' maths during science activities and don't understand that accuracy of measurement is an essential part of the question-and-answer sequence suggested here. Nonetheless, pupils will have to learn

19

Investigation One

Blocks of comparable size handled by pupils, put in order from the heaviest to the lightest and finally put in to a bowl of water to see if they floated or not.
Blocks were: wood (hard and soft), aluminium, iron, polystyrene, wax and glass.

The children noted their observations on a chart similar to this one:

Children decided that wood was not the only light substance that floats. I was satisfied that both weight and material had been considered as variables.

Investigation Two

Children handled thin sheets of metals and cooking foil. They tried to make floating shapes – boat shape emerged! I am not sure what they really understood – I think from discussions I had with them that they were now not so sure that all heavy things (metals) sank. They were beginning to feel that shape was important too.

	Sank	Partly sank	Floated on top
Wood (hard)			
Wood (soft)			✓
aluminium	✓		
Iron	✓		
Polystyrene			✓
Wax		✓	
Glass	✓		

Figure 2.3   A page taken from a class teacher's notebook

that there are various ways of presenting the data they collect from their experiments – for example, constructing tables, drawing graphs and diagrams. They also need to know when it is most appropriate to use a particular form of recording. Second-year juniors were examining the problems of streamlining and decided to record their results on a graph. When they found that they needed to collect more information about how long their boats took to travel the allotted distance, they investigated whether it was better to tow the boat from a pin above or below the hull. They were then able simply to add the information to their existing graph. They can now make many comparisons which they would have found hard to understand had they stuck to a series of tables for their results. Figure 2.4 shows the final graph produced by the pupils as part of their display.[3]

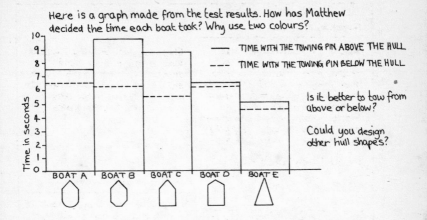

Figure 2.4 Some work done by second-year juniors at Blurton Primary School, Stoke-on-Trent

Having collected information resulting from their investigations, pupils may find it possible to give an explanation or answer to their original question. 'Trying to answer the question:' after designing and trying out different pulley systems children could understand why men working on a building site were using a wheel pulley system to help them haul large loads of bricks up to the second floor – it made the job easier! However, it is equally likely that pupils are no nearer an explanation after their original investigation, and this is the point at which teachers must realise that the idealised sequence of events must in reality be described as a cycle round which pupils may circulate several times. Depending on their particular problem or misunderstanding, it may be a case of merely checking on the accuracy of measurements or observations in order to enable a reinterpretation to take place. Perhaps the experiment they designed was not a fair test. There may be ways of altering it to make the test fairer: the variables may not have been controlled carefully enough or the initial investigation may not have been the best one to provide the answers the children sought. This is another occasion when teachers may find that schemes of workcards can come to their aid. Pupils can look at the same problem again and see if they

The framework for planning science activities

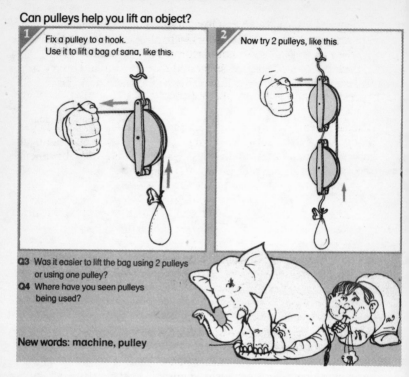

Can pulleys help you lift an object?

1. Fix a pulley to a hook.
   Use it to lift a bag of sand, like this.

2. Now try 2 pulleys, like this.

Q3 Was it easier to lift the bag using 2 pulleys or using one pulley?

Q4 Where have you seen pulleys being used?

New words: machine, pulley

Figure 2.5 Workcards such as these can help children solve problems (Source: 'Simple machines', card 69A, *Look: Primary Science*)

can understand it more easily after doing the activities on the card. The workcard shown in Figure 2.5 was one used by a teacher and pupils to enable them to learn about pulleys before they actually tried to tackle the problems generated by their visit to the building site.

The work shown here by 8- and 9-year-olds from Adlington St Paul's CE School, near Chorley,[4] illustrates again many of the points made previously. Each variable examined gave new evidence to help them answer their question 'How can we make a good parachute?'.

The corner shop beside Adlington St Paul's CE School, near Chorley, had a batch of toy parachutes which were soon snapped up. As stocks ran low children made their own. Some of the second-year juniors were puzzled and disappointed when their models did not perform well, so Lynette Cross, their temporary teacher, suggested that they should all try to design a good toy parachute. This was done in topic and craft time in one week, about 10 hours.

This is an example of pupils tackling a very practical problem. They are problem solving using inexpensive, easily obtained materials. In the case of this class, each variable was examined separately by a different group.

The children talked over the things they thought might make a difference to a parachute. They first proposed the material it was made of; later they thought of the size of the hole in the top and the weight hanging on the strings. With the teacher they worked out how to test these variables – one at a time – and then split into small groups to do the work. They gathered together again to assemble and discuss the results of each investigation.

The pupils were obviously alerted in the course of the class discussions to the different variables, but clearly, from their own accounts of the experiments, fair testing was something they considered very seriously. Figure 2.6 shows the results of an examination of each variable in turn.

By pooling their results, pupils had the opportunity to answer the question 'How can we make a good parachute?' and exclude design features which prevented their parachutes from performing as well as they had hoped.

This is where the distinction between science and technology becomes blurred, as Professor Paul Black pointed out in his lecture at the Standing Conference on Schools' Science and Technology: '...whereas the tasks we do in science are enquiry, the tasks in technology are about how can we meet this need, how can we solve this problem?'[5] The links he makes between science and technology are further explained in the diagram he uses, shown in Figure 2.7.

As long as we are aware that these links do exist, and that much of the experimental problem-solving activity that is advocated here will be crossing back and forth over the

Changing the fabric

Each pair of children used a different material.

We decided to make the test fair we would go
up to the gym and drop the chutes from the
climbing frame so that they all fell from the same
height.

We decided to drop each chute more than once
incase we did not drop the first one correctly.

I think the silk would float down the best.

Material used for Parachute	Time of descent in seconds
open net	1·1
close net	2
silk	28
cotton	15
nylon	1
cellular blanket	13
nappy	2
flannlette	2
plastic carrier bag	25
crepe paper	25
tissue	2
stiff paper	14
freezer film	28
bubble plastic	25

"I was surprised that the tissue chute fell so fast. I think it was too light to open properly.

The silk and the freezer film chutes were the best. To find the best time between them we dropped them from the top of the climbing frame 5 times. The freezer film chute fell the slowest."

Changing the weight

So far we have found out that the freezer
film parachute with the four cm hole is
the best design for our toy parachutes

We wanted to know what would happen
if we put more weights on the chute.

The only thing we changed was the number
of weights. We tested them the same
as before

Our results tell us that the more weights
we add on the faster the chutes fall down.

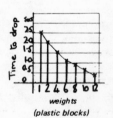

weights
(plastic blocks)

24

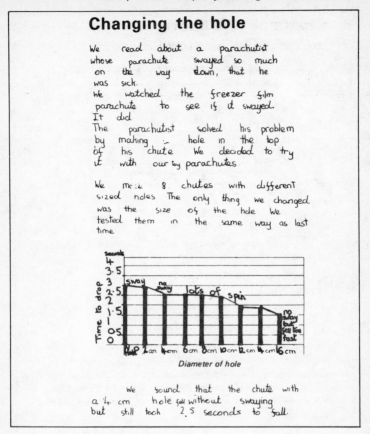

Changing the hole

We read about a parachutist
whose parachute swayed so much
on the way down, that he
was sick.
We watched the freezer film
parachute to see if it swayed.
It did
The parachutist solved his problem
by making ... hole in the top
of his chute We decided to try
it with our toy parachutes

We made 8 chutes with different
sized holes The only thing we changed
was the size of the hole We
tested them in the same way as last
time

Diameter of hole

We found that the chute with
a 4 cm hole fell without swaying
but still took 2.5 seconds to fall.

Figure 2.6 Testing variables
(Source: *Primary Science*, 12, autumn 1983)

science/technology divide, there is no further need for debate on
this subject in a book such as this. There are available several
resources that will explain and amplify the possibilities of
including technology within the primary school curriculum.[6]

What about pupils of different ages? Could we expect older
pupils to be more adept at planning investigations? In broad
terms, yes. However, don't underestimate the abilities of young
children – pupils that have been introduced to this scientific
way of working can, by the age of 8, be designing extremely

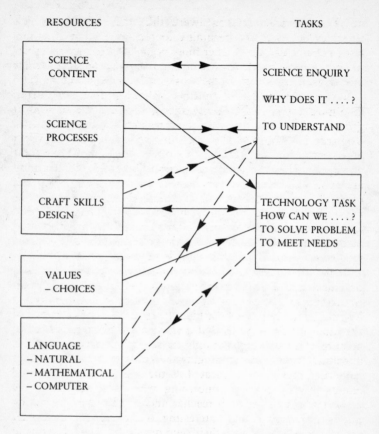

Figure 2.7 The links between science and technology
(Source: *Science and Technology in the Primary School*, Standing Conference on Schools' Science and Technology)

sophisticated experiments and controlling more than one set of variables. The sooner, the younger, a child begins to work in this way, the more benefit they will derive from it. These examples of infant science show how the beginnings of problem solving and controlling variables can be encouraged in any young pupils. Obviously the amount of teacher guidance required here is much greater as these pupils are not ready for the independent working that fourth-year juniors are capable of. These pupils are not aware that they are controlling variables but they are beginning to recognise what is a 'fair test'; nonetheless, the teacher must begin to introduce variables to her pupils in their attempts to find answers to their questions. This is seen in the work on bubbles in Figure 2.8.

If you have a class of fourth-year juniors that have never attempted any scientific investigations, you may indeed need to give more guidance and help them to sort out their fair tests. You may be disappointed in their first attempts, but it is worth persevering, for the freedom this offers pupils and their total absorption when they get used to controlling their own learning are quite addictive. They will want to work that way again and often. A detailed account of children's differences at various ages and stages of development can be found in sections 3 and 4 of *Approaching Primary Science.*[7] Those articles and others quoted in the bibliography will provide information about children's intellectual growth which is outside the scope of this book.

In the subsequent chapters on content choice and classroom organisation the setting up of various experiments and the roles of teachers and pupils during those activities will be explored at length. Asking questions – asking the right questions – is one of the most important skills that a teacher and her pupils need to acquire: it is important not only for scientific activities, but it is absolutely critical in encouraging the kinds of explorations that have been previously advocated. Returning to a problem raised earlier in this chapter concerning who asks questions, the answer seems to be, both teacher and pupils. Only by asking pupils provocative and interesting questions can a teacher encourage pupils to pose their own questions. Two chapters in the book *Primary Science: Taking the Plunge,*[8] edited by Wynne Harlen, are concerned with techniques of questioning. Sheila Jelly's chapter 'Helping children raise questions – and answering them' indicates ways in which teachers may be helped to improve their own questioning skills. She advocates three activities that individuals could try. The first involves analysing tapes of your own performance and the second scrutinising questions used in published workschemes and primary science materials – the main advantage suggested there is that the latter activity will heighten a teacher's awareness of possible types of question. The third and final suggestion is one that many teachers may already do subconsciously:

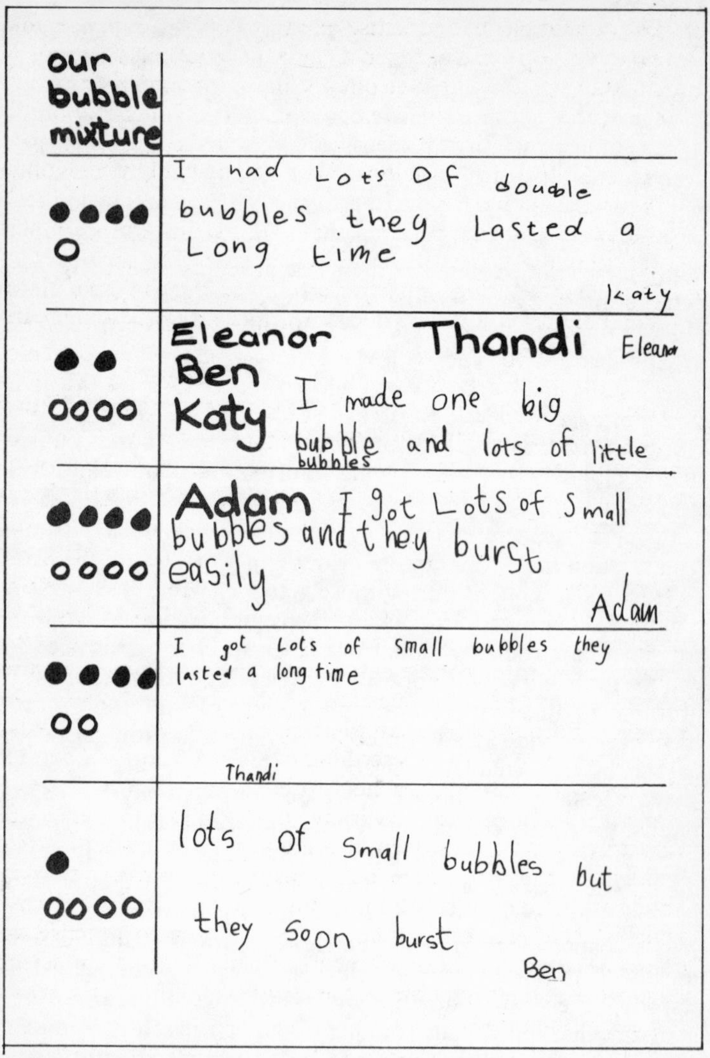

our bubble mixture	
●●●● ○	I had Lots Of double bubbles they Lasted a Long time Katy
●● ○○○○	Eleanor Thandi Eleanor Ben Katy I made one big bubble and lots of little bubbles
●●●● ○○○○	Adam I got Lots of Small bubbles and they burst easily Adam
●●●● ○○	I got Lots of Small bubbles they lasted a long time Thandi
● ○○○○	lots of Small bubbles but they soon burst Ben

Figure 2.8   Some work on bubbles done with 5- and 6-year-olds at Seabridge Infants' School. The children were examining the size and quantity of bubbles they made when they mixed different proportions of soap and water. The black dots signify water and the white ones soap.

Use odd moments to practise question-finding. Suppose, for example, you are waiting in a car park (a useful situation, since all schools will have one). What is its potential for science? What introductory questions could you ask about it to stimulate children's scientific activity? Make a list of attention-focusing questions. Try to go beyond the obvious properties such as colour/shape/size/kind/age and include questions involving patterns and relationships. For example: Which of the cars are rusting? Which parts of a car rust? Which parts have no rust? Do all cars rust in the same place? What attention-focusing questions might you ask about car types, windows or lights?

Stressing that as a worthwhile and productive activity will have a twofold effect: it will increase teachers' potential for exploiting their environment by extracting scientific explorations, and it will increase an individual teacher's confidence by building on skills that they already have.

The preceding chapter in the same book, by Jos Elsgeest, 'The right question at the right time', indicates a useful categorisation of the questions teachers ask. He talks about the difference between 'right' and 'wrong' questions and goes on to further categorise 'right' questions as 'measuring and counting questions', 'comparison questions', 'action questions' (or 'what happens' questions), and 'problem-solving questions'. Whatever classification is used for describing questions, categorising them is a useful exercise for teachers to engage in as it will help to increase the scope and variety of teacher/pupil dialogue. Constructive advice is given in the book in the form of lists of 'guidelines for productive questions'. During this discussion about asking questions we must not lose sight of our objective, which is that we want to encourage children to practise and enjoy scientific activities; we want to start the cycle of science advocated at the beginning of the chapter and that is the reason for asking questions.

So far, our concern has been with questions initiated by teachers – maybe in an attempt to encourage pupils also to question, but nonetheless teacher-inspired. What about children? Do they ask the right kind of questions? The answer is, yes, sometimes they do. Some third-year junior pupils noticed a house martin's nest above the door that led to their classroom.

They asked their teacher if they could find out how the nest stuck to the wall. As you can imagine, this one question led to a whole series of investigations: comparisons between mud, sand, earth and clay, and their various sticking properties. With the caretaker's help, they examined an old nest to see what clues they could glean from careful observations. The organisation in the school allowed the pupils to work in that way: it was a small village school with a high proportion of adults available to help and the parents were enthusiastic about participating and helping in any way they could. However, you cannot rely on pupils finding something to explore nor do many teachers like to work with that degree of spontaneity. Teachers have to provide a stimulating environment for their pupils and, through their own questioning skills, help their pupils to ask productive, absorbing questions – the 'right' questions, those that will lead on to fruitful activity. Again, there are many useful sources that teachers can read in addition to those already quoted.[9] But, as far as this book is concerned, how teachers encourage pupils to ask questions will be elaborated on during the course of the following chapter, which is concerned with more practical aspects of teaching and gives specific examples.

3

Planning what to teach: content choice

Once the basic framework within which a teacher can place science lessons has been established, the next problems to tackle are usually:

What do the children actually do?
Which topics to choose?
Are some topics more important than others?

Because these questions are prominent in the minds of many primary school teachers, this chapter on content choice comes early on in the book. The previous chapter gave us the bare bones (a guide to planning science lessons); this one will attach flesh to that skeleton. In order to do this I have examined the usefulness of existing published materials and highlighted examples of good practice. In this way it is hoped that teachers will find the necessary support in terms of resources and information to embark on scientific ventures of their own. The schemes used here were put together from a variety of sources. There is no shortage of good ideas in existing books of primary science; the problem for the teacher is more one of lack of time to amass or evaluate materials and ideas, and this chapter indicates some strategies that teachers can adopt.

Selecting the broad content of a science programme should not be an assignment for individual teachers to organise for their own class, mainly because it is very hard to make a choice of topics without reference to other colleagues in the school and without knowledge of the prior experiences of the children. Ideally, content choice should be made cooperatively by the whole staff and the best possible scenario would include the help of a special resource person, called a 'science coordinator' in this book, who has some experience to share with fellow members of staff and some detailed knowledge of the resources available to the school. The exact nature of this specialist role within the primary school and within science as a curriculum area will be explored separately in a subsequent chapter. Even though a cooperative, whole school approach has been advocated, do not feel put off if you are in a school where you are the lone voice of primary science – it is of course possible to go it alone and provide interesting scientific experiences for pupils, particularly as the science we have been discussing here is really a teaching method that is aimed at promoting a scientific way of working and not a specific set of activities. However, it is harder for a teacher to plan work without the help and advice of colleagues and pupils are certainly disadvantaged by such a disjointed approach to their learning.

Primary science is not content-bound: what topics are chosen for investigation are not as important as the teaching methods that teachers employ. If this is so, how do we ensure that the topics selected are going to give the children maximum benefit? Here the evidence gleaned from the APU Report *Science at Age 11* is usefully reiterated.[1] Remember, most primary school pupils at 10+ are found to be doing well at acquiring general skills which are important to their work in all areas of the primary curriculum, but they seem to perform less well in relation to the science-specific skills. While teachers are selecting topics for inclusion in their science scheme, some questions which were stated in the APU *Science Report for Teachers 1* should be uppermost in their minds. They relate specifically to science skills and will help teachers to evaluate the suitability of their choice in terms of whether it will provide the correct experiences for their pupils. Teachers must ask themselves whether the topic and the activities they select within it allow them the maximum opportunity to:

1   encourage children to design their own approaches to solving problems and allow them to try out their ideas

2   discuss with the children the progress of their investigations and encourage them to discuss with each other

3 discuss the children's results and challenge them to show how they were worked out from the evidence

4 listen to children's ideas and probe their 'wrong' responses; encourage them to explain their reasons for their ideas; use this knowledge in planning further activities for the children

5 help children to review critically their practical procedures and consider alternative strategies for solving problems or investigating.

None of this immediately or obviously suggests any particular topic, rather, it ensures that topics are chosen that allow the right kind of method to be employed. Further guidelines have been included here – these have been developed and agreed upon by experienced teachers and can also be used to ensure a varied and viable programme of activities. Topics chosen should:-

1 cover a wide range of subjects, e.g., air, energy, our homes, bubbles, sounds, the school pond, creepy-crawlies, bridges, etc. It is particularly important that as many sciences (biology, physics, chemistry, geology) as possible should be represented in this list.

2 be allocated to coincide with the known interests of particular age groups and should not be conceptually too difficult for the age or ability of those pupils. For example, the different classes' interests – in conkers, ball games or fashions in clothes – can be capitalised on and, although different age groups share some interests, particular playground activities are more absorbing to some age groups than others and such activities are admirable topics for scientific investigation. Topics that can only be tackled in an abstract way should not be attempted with primary-aged children. Examples of these would include descriptions of the mechanisms of photosynthesis or explanations of atomic structure.

3 reflect the strengths and interests of the teachers in the school. Staff members who are enthusiastic ornithologists,

photographers and rock collectors should be encouraged to develop resources for pupils' use, guide colleagues towards useful teaching materials and include their own expertise in the planning of the school scheme.

And, although this is not one of the criteria for selecting topics to study, the question of a simple and effective record-keeping system must be included in the overall planning. Some way of ensuring that each class or individual is not repeating the same topics must be included (the tadpoles-every-spring problem!), and this safeguard can also ensure that a wide variety of activities has been included. This is not entirely a separate problem from the one of recording pupils' progress, their strengths and weaknesses, but for the sake of a forward planning exercise, it has been treated as a separate issue. The record keeping that is being discussed here has evolved as a necessary part of a good planning technique.

A detailed study of a two-form-entry junior school comprises the bulk of this chapter and is intended to give practical and workable examples of curriculum planning, to show how selection of content took place, and to indicate how teachers with varied experiences used the basic framework to evolve their own particular lesson styles. The school described here was not exceptional in its resources, the teachers in the school had been teaching for differing numbers of years, and they had arrived at their qualifications through a variety of routes. However, they were all agreed that to promote science in the curriculum they would need support from each other and cooperation was enthusiastically advocated. In this brief description it is not possible to show all the frustrations and inevitable disagreements that occurred, nor is it appropriate to record the discussions, many of which were felt by the staff to have been invaluable. This account of one school's progress may therefore appear to have been remarkably painless. The necessary brevity of the account has helped to create this illusion, all sorts of upsets and mishaps did of course occur but in no way did the ensuing science that the pupils were involved in suffer.

Planning started from an initial list of science-related skills that were agreed by the staff:

finding patterns in observations
planning investigations/experiments
comparing
designing fair tests
controlling variables
predicting
giving explanations
hypothesising

Ideally, all topics, ideas for investigations, or anything called science, would have to incorporate and develop one or more of those skills.

The first serious entry into science activities by the school was in the form of a large project to which all the classes in the school could contribute. The question chosen to initiate the work was 'What is our school made of?' At an initial staff meeting a topic web was created. This covered a 6' × 3' wall (it only just fitted on) and included as many ideas as each member of staff could contribute. In fact, after it had served its initial function of stimulating discussion and getting every member of staff involved it was rolled up and relegated to the top shelf in a store cupboard! One book was particularly commended by the staff as a valuable resource during both the initial planning stages and the subsequent experimenting they undertook with their classes: Doug Kincaid and Peter S. Coles, *Houses and Homes*, from the series *Science in a Topic*.[2]

A shorter, barer version of the topic web, shown in Figure 3.1, became the new working document and the basis for further negotiation.

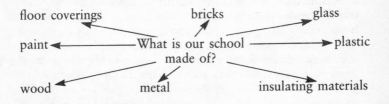

Figure 3.1 A simple topic web

Each class teacher claimed a topic and agreed to develop possible lines of enquiry, collect some necessary resources and then report back to a meeting. The staff agreed on a general format for the introduction of each topic to their class but beyond that, as long as they could reasonably demonstrate that their pupils were working on acquiring some of the specific science skills, their freedom to explore each topic was absolute. Each individual member of staff had demonstrably different strengths and weaknesses but each agreed that they were supported within that general framework.

Each class topic varied in the details of its development. These are given in outline to show how the autonomy of teachers can still be maintained within an explicit framework, an agreed method of working. Each of the teachers used the following list to help them in their planning.

1 All pupils explore the school and list and classify the variety of materials found on the premises. Obviously this preliminary reconnoitre would yield different results from each class.

2 The ensuing classwork would approximate to the following sequence of events:

   a) Discussing their own particular topic, establishing what pupils already know. Writing that down under the heading:
   'What do we know about glass/wood/metal/ etc.?'

   b) Framing the critical initial questions whenever applicable, e.g., 'Is all wood the same? What is the difference between the metal on our desks and that on the window frames?'

   c) Carrying out a preliminary sorting and classification of the materials the pupils are going to study. (This involves teachers in a lot of advance preparation.)

   d) Formulating of questions or problems which pupils will attempt to solve by designing their own experiments.

   e) Carrying out activities and evaluations.

   f)   Devising alternative strategies to gain more
        information, accuracy, etc.

3 Pupils must keep all pieces of work – each rough working,
    development of ideas, plan, sketch – in a group or personal
    folder so that detailed discussions about particular problems
    can take place with their teachers. It was envisaged that this
    would also help teachers in their future planning.
4 A final report would be produced, mounted and displayed
    in the main hall and pupils would explain their work in a
    presentation to the school, staff and parents at the end of
    term. (Although this did happen the staff agreed that it was
    too time consuming and did not warrant so much effort.)

    The actual development of work in the four junior years
is described in some detail.

Year One – insulating materials

Pupils were assisted by the school caretaker to climb a ladder
and peep into the roof space and they then described what they
saw:

   'lots and lots of white bubbles'
   'little white marbles'
   'tiny white stones'

With their teacher the class then investigated the polystyrene
granules. During the ensuing discussions their teacher coaxed
them towards a careful examination of their properties. They
tried to weigh them and found they had no scale sensitive
enough to weigh one small polystyrene ball. They all felt them
and noticed how they stuck together, and to them and their
clothes. They examined them carefully with a hand-lens. So far,
only further development of the children's general skills of
observing, describing, and writing has been outlined.

Some pupils knew that the granules were put there to keep
the school warm – they had them in their lofts at home. Their
teacher tried to develop the children's ideas on 'how to keep
warm' and 'what is meant by insulation' by broadening the
discussion away from the school's roof insulation. The teacher
asked the questions:

1	2	3	4
put a furry coat on it	put it in a hot bath	blanket feathers	put a woolly jumper on it
cover it with a blanket	put a woolly coat on it	hold it in your hand	cotton wool
			hamster bedding

Figure 3.2 Ideas for keeping the heat in a hot potato

'What do we know that keeps *us* warm in winter?'
'What keeps animals warm?'
'Do some things keep us warmer than other things?'
'How can we keep the heat inside a hot potato?'

This last question was introduced to stimulate the children into actually trying to design their own experiment. They had to write on a piece of paper what they would do to their potato to keep it warm. (This forward planning, designing, of an experiment is a critical part of the scientific method the teacher was trying to encourage.) The suggestions from four of the groups shown in Figure 3.2, reflected their own experiences – for example, the hamster and guinea pig owners suggested solutions they knew would work with their pets.

The children were encouraged to collect all the necessary coverings (although the teacher had a back-up supply in the scrap box) and then the children tried to investigate which potato kept the warmest. Their teacher introduced the idea of a fair test (or an unfair one in many cases) when the pupils could not agree on the 'winning' potato. The teacher helped them to list what was *not* fair.

1 Some potatoes were hotter than others to start with.
2 Some people put thick woollies on their potatoes and others didn't.
3 Some potatoes were bigger than others – no pupils were sure why this was a problem, but by now they were thinking all *differences* were not fair!

4   No one could agree on whether one potato was hotter than another to start with – how hot is hot?
5   Some parts of the classroom might be hotter than others.

They all agreed that in order to make their tests fair they had to

- use a thermometer to measure temperature (the teacher had first introduced them to one and shown them how to use it)
- use potatoes that were all exactly the same size (or as nearly as they could manage) or something else instead if that was too difficult. Jars of warm water were suggested.
- find out if big potatoes got cold more quickly than small potatoes
- wrap things up for comparable periods of time to give them a chance to see if they cool down.

The four groups all tackled a different problem this time, initiated by the class teacher after the previously reported discussion had taken place.

Group 1: Do big jacket potatoes or little jacket potatoes get cold quicker?

Group 1 used three potatoes and took the temperature of their potatoes by sticking the thermometer into the centre every ten minutes. (Initially they tried every minute but it got boring and they gave up!) Maybe they didn't learn much about the materials the school is made of, but they now know that if they are hungry and want to eat in a hurry it is better to choose two small baked potatoes than one big one!

Group 2: What keeps things warmest – woollen material, hamster bedding, hay or fur?

Group 2 were led towards using equal quantities of hot water in used washing-up liquid bottles and wrapping a different material round each one.

The group had difficulty trying to work out how to get the bottles full of water at the same temperature to start the race!

Group 3: What insulating material that you can buy for house roofs works the best?

Group 3 built small houses out of shoe boxes and covered the upturned lids to an equal depth with three different proprietary brands of insulating material. They put equal-sized mugs of hot water in the boxes and measured the temperature loss after half an hour. They generated a further problem – what about the walls?

Group 4: Do things keep warmer with more polystyrene bits around them?

Group 4 had considerable trouble with the sheer mechanics of this experiment – the polystyrene bits kept flying around. In the end they used different-sized boxes in which to place their mugs of hot water.
(Warning! The bits kept falling into the mugs of water – use jam jars with lids if you try this!)

We must not delude ourselves that the pupils thought out all these investigations for themselves. Their teacher had to ask them questions to set them on the right track to find solutions, but this work exemplifies clearly how deciding on content is only a starting point and that the most important things for a teacher to remember are to allow pupils to ask questions and make mistakes (within reasonable bounds of safety), and not to interfere too much – just sow some seeds of ideas and see how they develop. Also, this example of content development from a first-year class shows how critical the discussions between teachers and pupils are – the classroom must be organised to allow maximum interaction of this sort.

What was the teacher's advance planning? What did she take to the second planning meeting? First she devised a small chart, shown in Figure 3.3, showing the possibilities for experimentation, taking into account her pupils' capabilities.

These can clearly be seen to have been translated into actual activities, as the preceding explanation indicated. The teacher had anticipated that there would be four groups in her class and had tried to ensure four different lines of enquiry. Critical to her planning was also the collection of books, articles and examples of other teachers' work which (on her own admission)

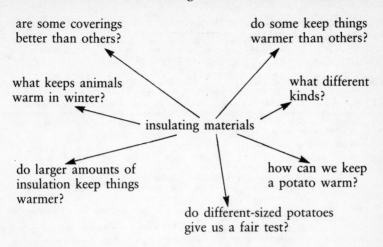

are some coverings
better than others?

do some keep things
warmer than others?

what keeps animals
warm in winter?

what different
kinds?

insulating materials

do larger amounts of
insulation keep things
warmer?

how can we keep
a potato warm?

do different-sized potatoes
give us a fair test?

Figure 3.3 Possibilities for exploring insulating materials

gave her the confidence to proceed![3]
  Her equipment list included:

1 bag polystyrene balls (insulation material)
5 lb bag of potatoes of various sizes
as many shoe boxes as local shoe shop would provide
5 thermometers
large collection of wrapping materials, to include:
  thin materials – cotton, nylon
  woolly materials to simulate fur
  old knitted garments
  cotton wool
  tin foil
bag of feathers (taken from an old pillow)
assorted plastic cartons and bottles

Year Two – bricks

The teacher with this year felt particularly anxious about
teaching science and lacked confidence. However, as the project
evolved, it became clear that her lack of confidence was
misplaced. She allowed her pupils to attempt activities that

Freida Rea, the class teacher, and Bill Surgeon, the Principal, report their work on this topic with a class of 8 and 9 year olds at Porter's Memorial Primary School, Belfast.

The children noticed that most local buildings were built of bricks. They also saw many clay pits and brick works marked on old maps of the area. At the largest brickworks in Northern Ireland, at Dungannon, they saw that bricks were made of sand, as well as clay, and were fired in a kiln.

Back in school we wondered what bricks would be like if they were not fired, and whether the kind of clay made a difference — would our local clay make a good brick? But what is a good brick? By questioning the children we drew out their ideas. It must keep out the rain, it must be strong and resist crushing, yet possible for a bricklayer to break if he needs half a brick.

Making our bricks

We made our bricks with clay from 4 different sources:-

1 — modelling clay from our local secondary school;
2 — Coalisland clay given to us at the brickworks in Dungannon;
3 — clay from Cushendun in the north, supplied by a parent who was a builder;
4 — local clay, found near the school.

The class was divided into 4 groups. Each group made 24 bricks with one of the clays, 6 of each kind shown in the Content column of this table.

For type B, 5 parts of clay were mixed with 1 of sand, as they did at the brickworks.

Type C was made *"because this was the way the people of Israel made bricks."* We mixed 10g of chopped straw with 1½ kg clay.

We made type D because *"we had found out that sand + lime + water makes mortar, which is very strong without being fired, and we wondered if 5 parts of clay + 1 part of lime would make a strong brick."*

In each case the children made a soft mixture with water, which they packed into moulds about 9cm long and of the same proportions as a house brick. We left the bricks to drain overnight, then finished off the unfired ones in the school oven at 100°C. We took the rest to be baked at 570°C in the kiln of our local secondary school.

We decided to give each brick a **code**

Number of Clay	Content	Test
1	A = Clay only	1. Permeability (F)
2	B = Clay + sand	2. Permeability (U)
3	C = Clay + straw	3. Crushing Strength (F)
4	D = Clay + Lime	4. Crushing Strength (U)
		5. Breaking Point (F)
		6. Breaking Point (U)

F = Fired. U = Unfired.

So e.g. 2B1 = a fired brick made of Coalisland CLAY + SAND which would be tested for Permeability.

How much water do they absorb?

All the weighed bricks were placed in basins of water for 30 minutes. They were then removed, dried with a towel and weighed.

The unfired bricks soon began to disintegrate so were removed and dried out again.

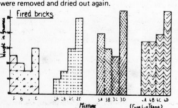

Fired bricks

Weight in grammes

Mixture (Fung Lin Tsang)

Least water soaked into bricks 2A, 2B and 1C, and most into the bricks with lime in them.

How fast does ½ml water soak in?

Syringe

We used a syringe to put ½ ml of water on each brick. Kok-Keung had a stop-watch and John wrote down the time it took for the water to sink into the brick.

Unfired bricks
All the clays + lime took the longest, 9 mins to 3½ hours.
Usually the clays + sand took the shortest time, 1½ to 3 mins.

Fired bricks
The water soaked in much faster, often in 10 to 20 seconds. The slowest were:

1A, clay 1 alone, 2 minutes;
2B, clay 2 + sand, 2 minutes;
1B, clay 1 + sand, 3 minutes.

Figure 3.4 Experimenting with bricks

CKS

"Crushability"

The children first thought of using a vice to crush the bricks, but *"the vice broke when we put the pressure on the second brick."* So they devised another method.

We looked for the highest brick building in Donegall Pass and we found one that has 300 bricks high This meant that the bottom brick had a load of 300 bricks on it Each of our bricks weighed 1/4 Kg so 300 bricks would weigh 75 Kg We wanted to know if our bricks would bear this load and some extra load for safety MR Surgeon's car weighed 900 kg so this would be about 225 Kg on each wheel This is three times the load we need

We drove the car on top of the bricks to see if they would crush

We took all the bricks which we wanted to test for crushing down to MR Surgeon car

Mr Surgeon's car

We put the bricks behind the rear wheels and backed the car on top of them Some were crushed. We used the car because we would not get enough weight any other way

Results:- The fired bricks that were crushed were 2D 3A 3B 3D 4C and 4D This shows that clay 3 is most easily crushed, and that clay + lime bricks are easily crushed also

Only one unfired brick was not crushed and that was 3C All unfired bricks with lime crushed to a powder except 2D Unfired bricks with straw did not break up so easily as the others

Breaking point

For this test the children used a guillotine which Peter designed and made at home. He fixed two vertical runners to a base board and nailed pieces of wood between them to keep them parallel. *"I fitted a piece of wood between the runners so that it slides up and down easily, and I fixed a bolster chisel to it with wire. Then I glued a scale marked in centimetres onto one of the runners, so I could see how far the bolster was dropping."*

Lee wrote *'We set each of the bricks at the bottom of the guillotine and dropped the bolster on them. We began at 20 cm on the scale and raised the bolster 2 cm each time until the brick broke.*

We did the same to the unfired bricks but began at 12 cm high as we thought they would break sooner."

Overall the fired bricks made with clay 2 were the strongest, and clay on its own made stronger bricks than when other things were added to it. The weakest bricks were those made with lime.

We found out...

1. That firing is important. Unfired bricks crumbled in water and were easily crushed and broken.

2. That our best brick was 2B(F). It was made of Coalisland clay + sand and fired, as at the brickworks.

   To find this we made a table of the best 10 results in each test, and then added up the scores of the different bricks. The best bricks, in order, were 2B and 2A, then, some way behind, 1B, 1C, 1A, 4A and 4B.

   Our local clay, 4, did not make good bricks but it was better than clay 3 from Cushendun.

3. That lime and clay is not a good mixture, it made the worst bricks.

We all agreed that it would have been better to have more than one brick for each test.

These tests, which tried to answer the questions we started with, were only a few of the ones the children did. They felt and looked at the different clays and saw how the different particle sizes settled into layers in water; they compared the effects of drying and firing on the size, heaviness and colour of the different bricks; they found the best way to remove stones from their clays; they discovered what happened when they mixed lime and water with clay or sand.

We were left with many other questions, such as:
What would happen if we changed the proportions of sand, clay or lime?
What if we changed the firing temperature?

This work was great fun for us all, children and teachers, and the fact that it involved many other parts of the curriculum, particularly mathematics and language, was an added bonus.

(Source: *Primary Science*, 8, summer 1982)

were extremely adventurous. She based her planning on a series of experiments outlined in ASE, *Primary Science* 8, summer 1982, and replicated some of the problems tackled by pupils at Porter's Memorial Primary School, Belfast. This is shown in Figure 3.4.

The class began their work by collecting as many different types of brick as possible. (In this parents and the obliging caretaker proved to be invaluable teacher's aides.) After careful observation of their collection, the teacher helped the children construct a list of properties that they thought were essential for bricks to make them efficient and effective building materials:

1 Some bricks have to be very strong and not crushable, but it should still be possible for a builder needing a half-brick to be able to break them.
2 Some bricks have to be very light.
3 Some bricks have to withstand high temperatures.
4 Bricks have to keep water out.
5 Bricks are different colours.

The teacher steered the class towards two properties that were finally selected for detailed study – strength and resistance to water. It was decided that these would be investigated in two ways: first, by using bits of manufactured bricks and testing their properties, and second, by using bricks the pupils had made themselves. By carefully altering the constituents of the different bricks they made, the teacher hoped to introduce them both to notions of fair testing and controlling variables. The class brick collection included:

common house bricks
breeze blocks
thermalite blocks
facing bricks
engineering bricks

Strength was the first property the class investigated and this time the teacher chose to include more class lessons in her organisational strategy. To encourage the children to think about fair testing, the teacher included all the pupils in a discussion about measures of hardness. The inevitable request to 'bash them hard with a hammer' was acknowledged as a useful exercise and in the playground, three bricks were selected for this treatment (beware – bits can fly about and it's better for observers not to get too close). Two different lines of investigation were finally decided upon: either to drop the bricks from a height or to drop weights on the bricks. The latter method was the one eventually employed. Each group of pupils worked on designing a weight-dropping device. After many elaborate suggestions, a relatively simple device proved to be the most effective and was the one they adopted. A large cardboard tube, 2 metres long, (the sort carpets are wrapped round in showrooms), was clamped over a metal plate leaving just enough of a gap to fit the various bricks underneath. Children could then release a known weight from the top of the tube and examine the effect that it had on each brick. Their class teacher claimed to lack confidence but ended up entering into some hair-raising activities that are certainly not to be recommended to the faint-hearted! The pupils had less opportunity to pursue their own ideas at this stage but were interested enough in the organised class work to become involved in extremely useful discussions about possible strategies for improving their experimental technique as well as trying, as a group, to interpret the results they got from the weight-dropping exercise. The pupils then went on to work in small groups where they had more opportunity to manage their own experiments.

These were the investigations relating to permeability of bricks and were similar to the two reported in *Primary Science*: 'How much water do they absorb?' and 'How fast does half a pint of water soak in?' But in this case, instead of using bricks they had made themselves, they used commercial bricks of different types. The pupils worked in groups of four with two bricks each and then compared their results on a large chart.

Depending on the resources of the school and the stamina of the class teacher, making bricks of their own using different ingredients provides an excellent opportunity for young children to work on the manipulation of variables. In this case the teacher did not introduce as many variables as in the examples in Figure 3.4. They used only one type of clay and added varying amounts of sand, lime and other, less usual, additives such as paints, pebbles and straw. These were ideas

45

that the children contributed. Once these bricks had been made, and some fired in the kiln in a local secondary school, the pupils were able to use tests similar to those that they had already devised for the manufactured bricks – this repetition and verification of scientific method is something that pupils will benefit from. Even the less confident pupils were able to tackle some of these investigations with real enthusiasm. They tested their own bricks for strength and permeability.

The teacher managing that set of investigations needed a greater structure than her colleague in Year One within which to work and for the staff meeting she provided the following outline, on which she subsequently based her classwork.

1 Examine exhibition of bricks
2 Establish strength and permeability as areas of study
3 Whole class watch 'brick bashing' exercise
4 Groups to write down suggestion for 'fair testing' to be vetted by teacher
5 Three bricks allocated to each group to allow investigations of strength
6 Introduce notion of damp course to permeability study
7 Two groups to use dropper method of measuring quantities of water
8 Teacher to set up demo of how damp course membrane works
9 Possible building of own bricks using model provided by ASE *Primary Science*, but not using different clays. Composition of bricks could include:

   clay + sand (different quantities)
   clay + lime (different quantities)
   clay + anything else the children would like to try

This is a different approach: more carefully structured and allowing the teacher the security of having less open-ended enquiry, but nonetheless giving pupils the opportunity to design their own experiments and encouraging a lot of discussion – something that is hard to portray here, though it was a very significant feature in that class.

This topic does need a quantity of inexpensive materials which were too bulky to store for future use:

variety of bricks
buckets of sand, lime and clay
assortment of weights
protective sheeting for classroom floor
large tubes from carpet shop
clamping mechanism

Other resources that were used in association with this topic are listed at the end of the book.[4]

Year Three – wood

The third-year pupils are of course a year older, and their class teacher is an experienced and enthusiastic science teacher – the coordinator for school science. She started off her class with two questions to bear in mind as they toured the school building: 'Is all wood the same? What are the differences?' From their observations, they drew up lists, charts and tables indicating

different colours
different noises when tapped
different surface appearance – grains in the wood (they used
a magnifying glass and took rubbings).

The children soon realised that they could gain only limited information about the wood from whole bits of furniture, floors, doors and window frames, and decided that they needed bits they could work with – break, take apart and float in water.

The teacher had already covered a table with scraps of different kinds of wood but more was solicited from DIY shops, parents, friends and a local timber yard. Once the collection was assembled few pupils could resist fingering a piece of wood as they passed the table and the comments came thick and fast:

'that feels smooth'
'didn't think that would be so heavy'
'what a dark colour'

These informal comments turned to a more systematic classification of the objects the class had collected and some time was spent in classifying, grouping and describing bits of wood.

The whole class participated in generating questions for investigations. This process is worth examining in some detail as it seemed so successful as a way of involving all the pupils and getting maximum cooperation between groups of pupils. The table with all the bits of wood was in the centre of the room and the pupils all grouped around it. The teacher called up a group of three pupils she knew would work together and picked three pieces of wood and asked them whether these different kinds of wood were all as hard as each other. Other class members were encouraged to think of ways they could find out about the property of hardness. After a few minutes' discussion the group was sent away with a sheet of paper that they had to complete: this would be the starting point of their investigations:

OUR SCIENCE PLAN

Names:

Our question:

How we **might** answer that question:

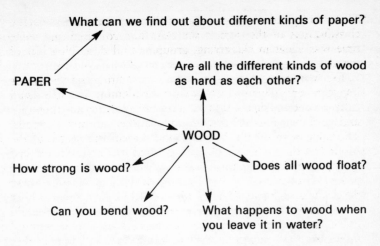

Figure 3.5   Topic web that emerged from class discussions

As each group devised their own questions, prompted by their teacher's initial stimulus, the teacher filled in a large topic web so that the children were aware of all that was going on. Figure 3.5 shows how the ideas developed in this case. Such a system gives the teacher flexibility to include any other ideas the pupils might think appropriate.

This teacher emphasised the planning of the experiments with each group and explained to her class that they were all looking for answers to their questions and that they might have to devise many different experiments before they could answer their questions. She shared her plan of action with her pupils and each had a copy of the resulting flow chart, shown in Figure 3.6, stuck inside the front cover of their science folder.

This is an example of where teachers have to be aware of the appropriateness of the tasks to their pupils' previous experiences and ability. Younger pupils would find it harder to decide what is a fair test and might be confused by the elimination of variables – they need much more guidance from their teacher. Many of these third-year pupils were able to attempt more sophisticated work, eliminate variables, define patterns in observations and even in some instances offer limited answers to their questions. Their teacher felt it a necessary part of their

49

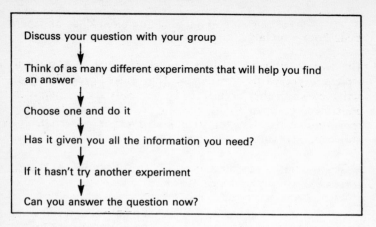

Figure 3.6   Flow chart for encouraging children to plan and evaluate their experiments

education to give them more responsibility for planning and evaluating their own investigations – hence the schema she shared with them.

The other major difference between the work done by this class and that produced in the others was that pupils used all their rough notes, and had to plan each experiment roughly on paper and store the plans in their files so that the teacher could use even those preliminary records to assess her pupils' progress.

The way in which this teacher stimulated her pupils into asking questions and subsequently guided them through the activities is of particular interest, and for that reason more space has been allocated to describing those activities. The pupils' recordings, their written explanations and attempts at answering the questions obviously varied enormously and for the sake of brevity have not been included here. The teacher presented the flowchart shown in Figure 3.5, 'Our science plan', the flow diagram indicating the proposed working plan, and her resource list[5] to the staff meeting. She emphasised the method she used and her attempts to give her pupils planning responsibility.

Year Four - metals

The two fourth-year teachers worked together to plan their topic and pooled their resources. They picked out a series of activities which they deemed to be necessary for all pupils to undertake for them to be able to understand some of the properties of metals before they embarked on their different investigations. These core activities were:

Classification – identification of different metals
Heaviness of different metals – relative densities
Where do metals come from – examination of ores.

They felt that there was, in this case, a body of necessary information that pupils needed to be familiar with to enable them to construct and carry out their own investigations. This is a clear departure from previous examples where teachers were not concerned that their pupils were engaged in specific fact-acquiring activities, rather that they were carrying out scientific processes. In fact, the contrast here is not as great as it seems at first. The preliminary exercises that the pupils undertook provided the base information from which they could then begin to raise questions. Their knowledge about the basic properties of metals was so slight that it was unlikely that their curiosity would even have been aroused without initial stimulus. This is an important general point to make about teaching science to young children. Preliminary fact-finding exercises or initial activities designed specifically to build up pupils' skills may be necessary before they can embark on discoveries of their own.

After the introductory exercises, discussions to stimulate questions took place. These were similar to those described previously, but with these older pupils their teachers were worried that they would not have the information necessary to guide their perhaps more knowledgeable pupils towards productive experimental work. They devised a topic web and collected materials from published schemes to match each possible line of enquiry. They felt this gave them sufficient back-up to make suggestions for experimental work to groups of pupils if they needed guidance.

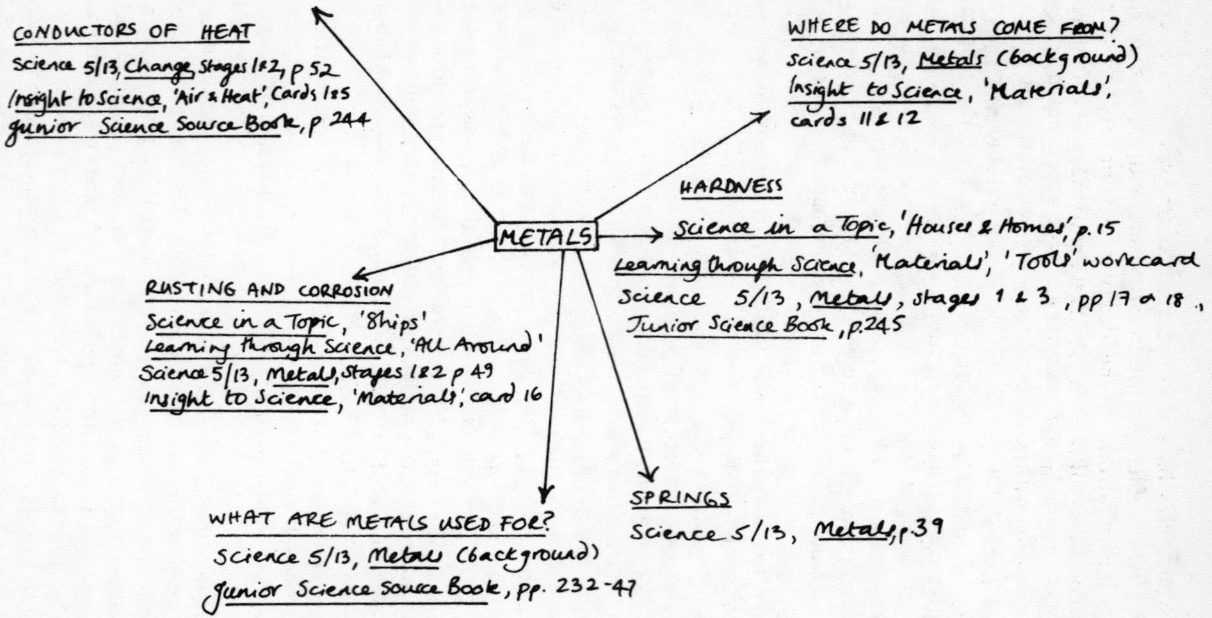
CONDUCTORS OF HEAT
Science 5/13, Change, Stages 1&2, p 52
Insight to Science, 'Air & Heat', Cards 1&5
Junior Science Source Book, p 244
WHERE DO METALS COME FROM?
Science 5/13, Metals (background)
Insight to Science, 'Materials', cards 11 & 12
HARDNESS
Science in a Topic, 'Houses & Homes', p.15
Learning through Science, 'Materials', 'TOOLS' workcard
Science 5/13, Metals, stages 1 & 3, pp 17 & 18.,
Junior Science Book, p.245
METALS
RUSTING AND CORROSION
Science in a Topic, 'Ships'
Learning through Science, 'All Around'
Science 5/13, Metals, Stages 1&2 p 49
Insight to Science, 'Materials', card 16
SPRINGS
Science 5/13, Metals, p.39
WHAT ARE METALS USED FOR?
Science 5/13, Metals (background)
Junior Science Source Book, pp. 232-47

Figure 3.7 Resource plan for the topic 'metals'

As well as this back-up system for themselves (illustrated by the flow chart referring to all the sheets and cards they had collected) they introduced the idea of a 'prompt card' which the pupils could have if they needed extra guidance – a sort of easy reference. An example of how this worked in practice came from a group of four who were trying to find a way of constructing a fair test to establish the relative hardness of different metals. They tried to design fair 'scratch' tests but found it impossible to devise another way of comparing the different metal sheets they were using. In this instance, the teacher gave them the prompt card with suggestions taken from Science 5/13, *Metals*, which, although it provided them with some information they did not already have, still required them to work out the details of their fair test.[6]

That class teacher also suggested that they investigate the relationship between bouncing and hardness (again as suggested in *Metals*, Stages 1 and 2) but didn't give them a written card this time. Instead they engaged the group in an extended discussion and thus led them towards constructing apparatus similar to that described on page 32 of that resource book.

Unfortunately, it is impossible in the short description of this approach to teaching primary science to do justice to the enormous collection of resources both for their own use and their pupils' that the teachers amassed before embarking on the topic. They did voice the anxiety that their rigorous forward planning had perhaps made them less sensitive to the pupils' own imaginative solutions to some problems but suggested that after the first run of the topic they would have the confidence to allow more flexibility in the future.

From the work that class did – which corresponded quite closely to the topics included in the original chart – some problems and developments arose which are worth mentioning here.

Some particular misconceptions that the pupils had could be avoided by selecting the samples of metals very carefully. For example, some pupils were unaware that aluminium was found in anything but sheets! It would be essential to have samples of the same metals in different forms e.g. blocks, lumps, sheets, wires, and household or manufactured objects.

This topic, like all the others done in the school, was very clearly linked to the environment and to helping the pupils

Hardness Test

If you're having problems devising a fair test to compare the hardness of metals, think about this idea.

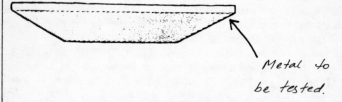

Metal to be tested.

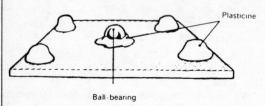

Plasticine

Ball-bearing

The Plasticine holds the ball-bearing in position and prevents the plates from rocking whilst putting them in the vice

1. What is the ball-bearing for?
2. What use are the lumps of plasticine?
3. What do you expect to see on your piece of metal after you have tested it?
4. Can you use this idea if you don't have <u>sheets</u> of metal?
5. Can you change the ideas here to suit your experiment?

Figure 3.8   Prompt card used to help pupils devise a test for hardness
(Source: *Metals*, Stages 1 and 2, *Science 5/13*)

obtain more information on the world about them. Each property of the metals that they investigated was carefully related to everyday usage.

The 'hardness of metals' investigations and the findings of that group led on to discussions about manufactured goods and their durability. Rusting and corrosion investigations led on to further work (undertaken after school and during lunch-breaks) on effective ways of protecting metals used out of doors. Heating metals and work on conductivity resulted in a survey of the constituent parts of household appliances.

The resources needed to carry out this work fall into two main categories; firstly, books and other paper materials, and secondly, the equipment collections of metals and other apparatus. A comprehensive list of the first can be found in Figure 3.7 and a resource list for the second would include:

sheets of metals
metal blocks[7]
wire – different thicknesses and made from different metals
a large 'junk' collection of various metallic objects, e.g., old nails, hinges, tin trays, toast racks (this collection can be enormous)
any old kitchen appliances that can be taken apart
small metal balls (ball-bearings and metal marbles).

What do these four examples of the science activities in junior classes show us? The most important point to emerge is that despite the very different teaching styles and experiences of the teachers concerned, they found it possible to agree upon the need for an experimental, 'hands on' approach to teaching science. In the main, the activities that they selected with their pupils encouraged them to ask questions and provided an opportunity for specific scientific skills to be practised. Eight different teachers each contributed from their own strengths to find ways of planning topics and selecting appropriate content for their pupils. The staff planned and coordinated their teaching method and then fitted appropriate content into that scheme, looking all the time for suitable vehicles to enhance the growth of scientific skills in their pupils. Both experienced and inexperienced staff found that decisions relating to content could be made more readily when there was a clear indication of the desired teaching method.

However, the whole-school topic approach is not one that most teachers would want to adopt all the time and, in the case study described, was one that the staff only embarked on once a year. A different topic was chosen each year, thus creating a four-year cycle:

What our school is made of
Ecology of the school grounds
Traffic and transport
Energy

The advantage of this was that all the valuable resources collected could be reused and periodically updated. There was a very specific effort to maximise assets: resource collecting is time-consuming and should be a once-off activity. The teachers also recognised the benefit that they and the children gained from such a large-scale cooperative venture. Parental involvement was an important feature of this type of activity as not only were the parents invited to a final display and explanatory session but they were also asked to help teachers and pupils at various times during the term.

How else was content determined and what other topics were included? Staff used the same criteria that they had previously agreed upon to select explorations and topic areas that they would like to undertake with their classes. This resulted in a long list (Figure 3.9) being produced.

Each child had a copy of this list placed in their file when they entered the junior school and topics were ticked off as they were completed. With that system, any class teacher could see at a glance what activities their new pupils had attempted in previous years. There was no attempt made in that exercise to evaluate the quality of each pupil's work – this document was designed to ensure that each pupil had a varied and well balanced science diet. The list reproduced in Figure 3.9 looks very brief and that was part of its success. It was not time-consuming for the teacher and it prevented pupils from repeating topics. Teachers could also add topics to the list that the children had 'acquired' during the year – these may have arisen out of pupils' interests, local events or stimulated by television or radio programmes.

In addition to the topic list there was a science folder, kept in

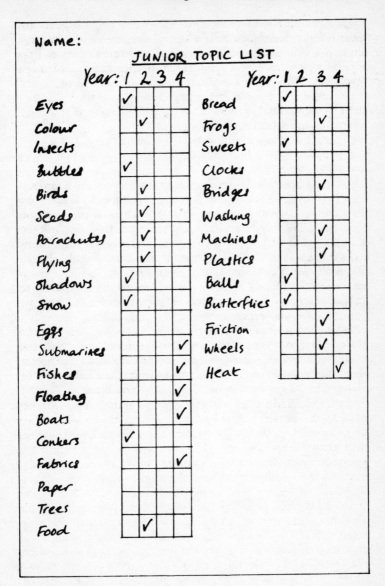

Name:

JUNIOR TOPIC LIST

	Year: 1	2	3	4
Eyes	✓			
Colour		✓		
Insects				
Bubbles	✓			
Birds		✓		
Seeds		✓		
Parachutes		✓		
Flying		✓		
Shadows	✓			
Snow	✓			
Eggs				
Submarines				✓
Fishes				✓
Floating				✓
Boats				✓
Conkers	✓			
Fabrics				✓
Paper				
Trees				
Food		✓		

	Year: 1	2	3	4
Bread	✓			
Frogs			✓	
Sweets	✓			
Clocks				
Bridges			✓	
Washing				
Machines			✓	
Plastics			✓	
Balls	✓			
Butterflies	✓			
Friction			✓	
Wheels			✓	
Heat				✓

Figure 3.9   An example of the junior topic list for a third-year junior pupil

the staffroom, where each teacher gave a more detailed account of each topic they taught. Flow charts were developed for each one, on which the activities undertaken were noted as well as an indication given of the skills the children had been practising. The science coordinator in the school had the job of overseeing the science activities and helping with their development when it was appropriate – this is something that will be returned to in later discussion.

Choosing content need not be a frightening task. Once rules and guidelines have been agreed amongst staff and sufficient safeguards built into the system to prevent repetition and to encourage science skills development, most topics are appropriate. This chapter has shown that how work is tackled by children of different ages is more important than the selection of subjects to study. Primary science guidelines put out by different local authorities give concise and useful suggestions for helping teachers to select content[8] and there are also books like Alan Ward's *A Source Book for Primary Science*, which teachers will find full of useful ideas.[9] In my experience, once teachers start to include science in their class activities, the problem soon becomes one of selecting what to leave out rather than what to include.

The collection and management of resources are important issues that are very closely associated with the kinds of choices that teachers make regarding science content, and this will be explained in the following chapter.

4

The organisation of science within the primary curriculum

Teachers have to decide how science is going to be included in their planned curriculum. Is science going to be separated from other primary school subjects and studied in discrete packages or will the school policy be to subsume science activities within topic or project work? (Many primary schools do organise their pupils' work into topics that attempt to cross subject boundaries but whether this is a desirable or efficient way of educating primary-aged pupils is not our main concern here.)

However, what is important to establish is to what extent science teaching and learning, in the way that it has been described in previous chapters, as an experimental, investigatory activity, will be affected by either separating it from or integrating it with other curriculum areas. Is an attempt at integration the best way of ensuring that those specific scientific skills that have been named repeatedly throughout this book are to be acquired, used, practised and built upon with all pupils? Or would science be better taught as an activity clearly set aside from all others where specific goals could be aimed at and objectives reached? This debate is one that produces emotional responses from teachers and it is important to remember again how critical personal biographies are to the formulation of ideas about the appropriateness of any particular teaching style. A teacher trained in the immediate post-Plowden era may be much more inclined to favour a model where science arises from general topic or interest work, whereas someone who feels uncertain of their own expertise in science and is particularly lacking in confidence in an open-ended, experimental situation may feel that they can cope more easily with a less flexible approach – one where science appears on the timetable as 'Science', with clearly spelt out aims and objectives. Separate science or science as part of topic work? That question indicates a polarity or exclusivity of opinion. I have done that deliberately in order to highlight certain points, although, realistically, such extremes rarely occur in practice.

Separate science

What are the implications and knock-on effects of organising science as a clearly defined separate activity? As intimated earlier, it may well be one way of encouraging otherwise reluctant teachers to tackle unfamiliar activities, particularly as these activities can be selected (and this has been explicitly stated in many published schemes) to build on certain skills and provide a set of structured and sequenced experiences for pupils. Figure 4.1 shows part of the index of *Look: Primary Science* where a specific sequence of experiments is suggested.

One of the unintended consequences of this form or organisation may be that it becomes less easy to make cross-curricular links and therefore science may become isolated and less immediately relevant to the children. If a set amount of time has been allocated for science activities every week there is a possibility that teachers pre-plan so rigidly in order to maximise their science allocation that they lose sight of the importance of allowing children to carry out their own experiments and make mistakes. It is more difficult to feel relaxed about the absence of an end product (i.e., the completion of an experiment or task) during a particular lesson if the pupils will only be doing science again next week. Just because science is timetabled does not necessarily mean that it becomes content-bound, but this is a possibility, and if teachers favour this way of working because it affords them more security then there is a distinct chance that the best of primary science, as advocated throughout this book, will not emerge. There is no sinister conspiracy suggested here, merely a warning that by a seemingly simple act of timetabling to ensure science its place in every child's activities, it may be difficult to sustain a truly experimental approach which enables pupils to explore their environment and develop a questioning mind.

Figure 4.1 (Opposite) A sequence of experiments
(Source: *Look: Primary Science*, Teachers' Guide A)

Water

23A FLOATERS AND SINKERS

Some objects float in water; others sink but may be made to float by hollowing them out.

Which objects float?
Can you make sinkers float?
How well does a straw float in oil?

24A GOING DEEP

Water presses on objects in it; the pressure increases with depth.

As the frog dives deeper what changes does he feel?
Can you make use of water pressure to spin a bottle?

25A WATER ON THE RUN

Water flows until its surface reaches a common level.

Does water run downhill?
Does water spread out?
What does water do in a U-tube?
Can you make a siphon?

26A WATER'S SKIN

The surface of water acts like a stretched skin and it can support objects. The surface also sticks to some objects.

Can you float a pin on water?
Can you see detergent weaken the skin on water?
Will the skin move a boat?

27A DISSOLVING THINGS

Some substances dissolve in water; others do not, but may dissolve in other liquids.

What happens to coffee powder in water?
Does everything dissolve in water?
What makes sugar dissolve faster?

28A FULL TO OVERFLOWING

An object which sinks in water displaces a volume of water equal to its own volume.

What will a beaker hold?
Can overflowing water be useful?

Planning experiments and carrying out investigations are time-consuming activities which are not always neatly parcelled up into allotted amounts of time. Pupils may not have enough time to make mistakes. The timetabling must, by implication, necessitate more teacher-led activities, which are not in themselves harmful but might in an extreme case lead away from hands-on activities for pupils. It is perfectly possible for exciting child-centred activities to go on at regular weekly intervals in the same way that maths and language are taught in measured doses, but it is harder to sustain spontaneity and maintain a continuity between different science topics. All these points are summarised in the following table.

Table 4.1 Some implications of science being taught as a separate subject

Advantages	Disadvantages
• Easier to ensure that some science takes place on a regular basis	• Possibility of allocating too little time for experimentation because of all the other time-table demands
• Individual pupil's progress more easily recorded	
• Development of skills can be more easily managed and monitored	• Tendency for too much 'teaching' to go on to maximise time allocation
• May be an easier way for an inexperienced teacher to work.	• Danger of being bound to plans or published schemes of work
	• Harder to relate science activities to other curriculum areas
	• Difficult to be spontaneous and capitalise on science arising from an unusual occurrence
	• May not allow enough time for pupils to make mistakes.

Science as part of topic work

Before debating the merits or disadvantages of including science activities within topic work, some brief discussion is necessary of what could exist under the general rubric of topic work, and here two different scenarios will be considered. The first is one in which all activities (except mathematics and language work) are organized under the umbrella of a topic – the theme links humanities, science, art and craft, and other areas of the curriculum. With such an arrangement, there would be a specific effort made to blur the distinctions between different subjects. Such a scheme is shown in Figure 4.2.

The possibility of capitalising on pupils' interests and providing the opportunity for pupils to spend varying amounts of time on particular aspects of the topic are more likely to occur within this inevitably more flexible timetabling arrangement. However, there are distinct dangers inherent in allowing science to emerge as one strand from a multi-disciplinary topic. It may well be that the sort of investigations that emerge from such a form of organisation are not very fruitful; it may even be a case of squeezing in some science just to make sure it has appeared! Monitoring of pupils' work and keeping records of completed activities will also be more difficult unless some conscious effort is made to overcome this problem.

An interesting example of the discussion carried on in a school relating to the place of science within the general framework of topics is found in *Developing Pupils' Thinking Through Topic Work: A Starter Course*.[1] This book, published under the aegis of the School Curriculum Development Committee, includes a case study of a school, Dovecote Mill Primary School. The extract from the transcripts of discussions held between the researchers and members of the school staff reflect the headteacher's anxiety about including science in topics and indicate some of the problems that may be encountered when there are differences of opinion amongst the staff:

> I am having a little battle at the moment because at one time, when we first accepted the *Look-Science* scheme, the Notts. scheme, it was great because we were all enthusiastic. We had a science period in the timetable and we did science as

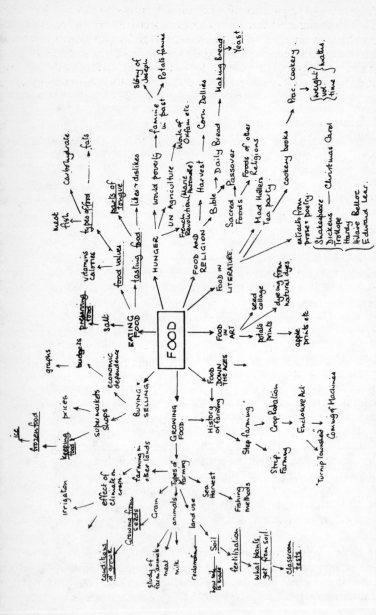

Figure 4.2 A topic web showing some work planned by a first-year junior teacher. This is a general scheme linking all curriculum areas; the science aspects of the topic have been underlined.

science. I could see science and I could see a progression: some kids doing experiments with air or electricity or water. Now the staff say they prefer the science to go in with the general topic and interest work and I feel we have lost it. I feel now it's become just part of the mishmash of the history and geography and environmental studies even though at any one time in the year one class will do a particular science topic.

Although that is an opinion expressed by a particular headteacher, it reflects common anxieties associated with the inclusion of science in general topics.

The second possibility when considering topics as a vehicle to teach science is to use a much less broad-based topic – one with a scientific bias: by this I mean topics that begin from a particular scientific investigation, lead on to other explorations and experiments, and yet still allow teachers to make links with other subjects. In this way the science work can be structured sufficiently to enable teachers to feel confident that their pupils are building up their skills and also allow for the likelihood of linking the science they do with other areas of the curriculum. Figure 4.3 gives an example of this type of topic.

In this example of an infant teacher's work with her class there are clearly defined 'scientific' areas – insulation and bubbles – that lead into possibilities for creative writing – flames, colour puddles and rainbows. Group work on some simple mathematics could arise out of cars, clothes, visibility tests and the survey work on common colours. The emphasis of a topic like this one is certainly on science activities but it in no way precludes excursions into other subject areas. This same teacher complemented her scientifically based activities with a separate topic based on the study of folk tales, a theme around which art and craft, history and geography was linked. Clearly any science extracted from that theme would have been very unsatisfactory.

Another advantage that may ensue from science within a topic – and this is an organisational point that will be pursued in a later chapter – is that if a topic is organised so as to provide a variety of activities, including non-scientific ones, some pupils can work independently of the teacher some of the time, and the teacher can spend a good proportion of her time

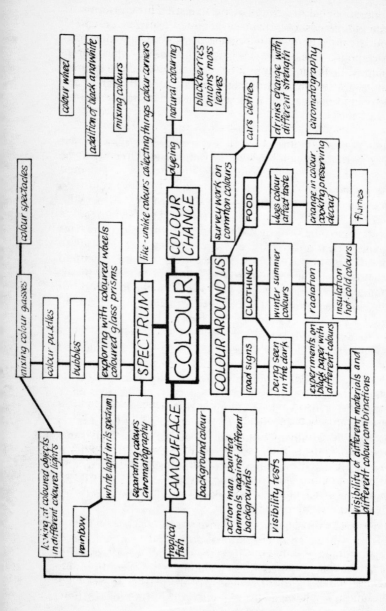

Figure 4.3 Flow chart of a topic with a scientific bias (Source: *Primary Science Guidelines*, Cheshire County Council)

with the individual or groups doing science. Those discussions between individuals and their teacher that have been described previously can be more easily organised within that framework. All the points relating to science and topics have been summarised in the following table, but it must be emphasised that as two different interpretations of topic work have been offered, some of the points may have more relevance to one than the other.

My feelings about the place of science in the curriculum are that, as topic and project work are well established in the primary curriculum and science is the relative newcomer to many schools, it is by using familiar vehicles such as topics that science has a good chance of getting established in the primary curriculum. Broad-based topics present too many pitfalls but, on balance, I think that the great advantages to be gained by including science in the primary school can be ensured by a wise and careful choice of scientific topics, planned around specific scientific aims and including excursions into other areas of the curriculum. With this in mind, here are some suggestions for the sort of topics that might be selected and some indication of time allocation within the total curriculum.

1 One large-scale science project lasting throughout a term – perhaps as part of a whole school venture as described in chapter 3
2 At least one smaller science topic in each of the two other terms
3 Some problem-solving activities linking science, craft and design – loosely termed technology
4 Small investigations set up to capitalise on any incidents that occur in the school. (For example, pupils kept slipping on one particular bit of flooring and that led to an investigation into floor surfaces.)
5 Pupils' particular interests should also be encouraged. (A child who was interested in tropical fish might be led towards an investigation of streamlining.)

The advantage of doing one large-scale project lasting a term is that it enables members of staff to cooperate, build up confidence as part of a team and collect resources with the help of colleagues. When the whole school engages in something like

67

Table 4.2 Some implications of science taught within topics

Advantages	Disadvantages
• Science *content* alone not so easily mistaken for science – process approach encouraged	• Uncommitted teacher could avoid experimental science
• More flexible timetabling allows pupils time to make mistakes and experiment	• Record-keeping more difficult
• More opportunity to relate science to other aspects of the curriculum	• Could spend too long on science – an overenthusiastic teacher may neglect other curriculum areas
• Spontaneity more likely, thus able to capitalise on an unusual occurrence	• Individuals may not be engaged in entirely appropriate activities – harder to monitor
• May allow teachers more time to work with individuals on science if the whole class is not involved with experimentation.	• Topics may be too broad or general to initiate successful experimental work.

this it has the added advantage of showing the pupils (by example) that science is a worthwhile activity – it gives it an importance in the school curriculum. But if the organisation of the school does not allow for such a cooperative venture – and there is no doubt that the organisational problems of such an activity can be very time-consuming and may not be to your school's best advantage – I would still like to suggest that an individual class could tackle one large project each year. The example I used in chapter 3 could form the basis for such a series of activities. However, I have found that any such project should not usually last for more than one term. By that I do not suggest that this should be the only topic undertaken during that term, but that, no matter how the teacher (or teachers) choose to organise their work, be it on one afternoon a week, one day a week or in bursts of a few days at a time, pupils should move on to different science activities at the end of the term. With young pupils of primary school age it is essential that we keep firmly in mind the skills and processes that are an essential ingredient of learning and practising science, and, although the same skills need rehearsing many times before pupils become proficient at them, it is equally important to practise those skills in different circumstances. An example of this can be found in a group of pupils who were investigating the property of hardness of material within the context of 'What is the school made of?'. They struggled initially to produce a fair test so that they could compare the properties of different kinds of wood and they then moved on to test bricks, mixes of cement and finally different kinds of plastics. In each case, they devised a test for hardness, but, after the initial struggle, the pupils developed a set routine: either they dropped a heavy object on the test articles or they tried to break them by hanging or placing heavy weights on them. I am not decrying the value of this exercise, only pointing out that after the first few attempts it had outlived its usefulness. Those pupils needed to move on to new challenges to break out of their established routine and practise their newly acquired expertise at planning investigations by tackling a completely different question or problem.

During each of the other two terms, a science-based topic of shorter duration could be included as part of the pupils' work. If a record-keeping system similar to the one advocated in the previous chapter is adopted by the school it can provide teachers with sufficient freedom to select topics they feel familiar with while at the same time ensuring some continuity between classes and avoiding the danger of repeating popular topics too often.

The summer term is really the most appropriate time to undertake some kind of ecological study. Many primary science schemes have useful ideas to enable teachers and pupils to plan experiments and undertake investigations associated with the natural sciences;[2] these have perhaps replaced the traditional junior school nature table. These investigations need not include trips to field study centres (although these can be very worthwhile expeditions) and can be very simple, short-term projects. Figure 4.4 is an extract from a teacher's planning notebook giving some indication of the scope and range of the

THESE ARE SOME INVESTIGATIONS THAT
HELPED US TO FIND OUT ABOUT PLANTS AND
ANIMALS

SEEDS

1. We made a collection of as many seeds
   as we could find. We found out where
   they came from.
2. We soaked some seeds in water and
   observed what happened to them.
3. We compared how quickly seeds showed
   the very first sign of life.
4. We made a graph of the different rates
   of growth of different seeds. (We used
   4 kinds - pea, bean, corn and cress.)
5. We planted seeds in different sorts of soil
   to see how they grow.
6. We planted pea seeds at different depths
   in tall plastic measuring cylinders to see if
   the small shoots can push their way through
   different depths of soil.
7. We planted bean seeds all different
   ways up to see if there is a right way
   of planting them.

WEEDS

1. We decided what the difference was between
   a weed and other plants.
2. We dug up 5 different kinds of weeds to
   look carefully at their roots.
3. We chose some weeds with long roots
   and tried to measure how hard we had
   to pull before we either got them out of
   the ground or the tops snapped off - we
   used a spring balance for this.
4. We kept a daily diary of a small patch
   of grass and weeds to see how quickly
   everything grew after it had been mown.
   We noticed if it rained or not.

CREEPY CRAWLIES

1. We looked carefully under loose bricks to see what animals lived there. We counted each sort and then put the bricks back.

2. We collected some woodlice and gave them choices of wet and dry and light and dark places to live to see which they preferred.

3. We looked carefully in the hedgerow to see how many insects and spiders we could find.

4. We compared different kinds of spider webs. We made our own with wool and card.

5. We found out where worms like to live.

Figure 4.4 A list of investigations undertaken by 9-year-olds

investigations she attempted with her pupils.

Teachers can include some problem-solving activities in their class scheme. When children are carrying out investigations and experimenting, they are to a certain extent solving problems: the science work in this book has been built up around a notion of asking and trying to answer scientific questions. What is advocated here is that the pupils should also work on problems, either introduced by the teacher or initiated from their own experience, that link science, craft and design, and simple technology. By technology I mean finding an actual physical solution to a problem using scientific skills and know-how acquired during the pupils' craft and design experiences. Pupils will be engaged in making working models and building constructions and in each case testing the effectiveness of their solutions to their particular problem.

Problem solving can be tackled in a variety of ways. The two examples given here show pupils using, in the first case, manufactured construction equipment (this may be beyond the pocket of some schools) and the second shows different possibilities using a small amount of bought materials and a considerable amount of collected 'junk'.

Third-year junior pupils were using Lego Technic to explore the basis of model construction. The workcards included with the sets introduced them to the basis of, among other things, using gears, motors and pulleys. After they had worked with the Lego for some time, the teacher introduced the pupils to a problem.

> Construct vehicles and test them to find the one that will travel the furthest along the floor after it has been launched from the top of a small ramp.
>
> You may only use the pieces from one Lego Technic box.

Then the children worked in groups. They were concerned with the mechanics of putting together a vehicle that was sturdy enough to travel down a ramp and along the floor; at the same time they had to make decisions about the size and the surface texture of the wheels, and the general shape and size of their vehicle. All these variables had to be tested by building and rebuilding the model vehicles and this involved pupils in design work. Whether they write this stage down or do any pre-planning on paper, is up to the individual teacher, but these are good habits to establish both for science and design education.

The pupils then needed to evaluate the success of their attempts through a testing programme. All of this is excellent science or good craft and design – or is it technology at a simple level? Probably all of these: here the primary curriculum and the ethos of primary education allows for the blurring of distinctions between subjects. This extension of problem-solving into design and technology provides another way for pupils to try out their developing experimental skills using different mediums.

Another strategy, developed very successfully by a teacher in a Stoke-on-Trent primary school is that of initiating problem solving through storytelling. Obviously any story will do, and Figure 4.5 gives an example of one they have used to great effect.

The materials the pupils use to meet the challenges in the story can depend on the emphasis teachers wish to put on the work. Someone with CDT expertise would be more inclined to provide and use more specialised equipment such as tools of different kinds and various sorts of wood, whereas another

Once upon a time there were two children named Jim and Mabel. They were brother and sister and lived in a very old house with their parents in the far north. It was a wild and dangerous place to live but they were sensible and clever children.

News came to them that a terrible dragon was terrorising the countryside causing havoc and bother where ever it went. It was so bad that the king offered a large reward for the capture of the dragon. The children decided that they would earn this reward and so early one morning they set out to capture the dragon.

Before they had gone very far they had a shock. During the night a storm had blown away the bridge over the gorge. Without wasting any time the children made a structure and got across the gorge (they were clever children).

PROBLEM ONE

- Construct a bridge to cross a gap of 50 cm. The roadway must be at least 5 cm wide.
- You must make your bridge out of the 2 sheets of card provided.
- Your bridge should support a weight of 250g.

They walked for many miles and entered a dark wood. Before long the children came to a strange cottage made of sweets and chocolate. They entered the cottage and were captured by an evil old witch and put to work washing up and doing the housework. When darkness fell they escaped from the witch by driving off in her magic car but before they went Jim took a Mars Bar to eat on their journey.

After leaving the wood the children found themselves outside a castle wall. If they wanted to carry on with their journey to capture the dragon they must get over the wall and safely down on the other side. Being clever children they soon managed this.

PROBLEM TWO

- Design and construct a device for getting the Lego figures over the castle wall *SAFELY*.
- The wall will be 30 cm high.

By the side of the road were the ruins of buildings destroyed by the dragon. They were not afraid and strode on. As they turned a corner in the road they saw the dragon coming towards them. It was huge and fierce. They hid in the ruins as the dragon went by. During the night the children constructed a trap and waited patiently for the dragon. Soon along it came and BINGO! they captured it.

PROBLEM THREE

- Design and construct a trap to capture the dragon. You must measure the dimensions of the dragon before you begin.

Soon after the children collected their reward and set off home to give their parents the good news. They got home just in time for tea.

But what about the dragon? The king found out that a rich man in America collected dragons so he was sent to America where he lived happily ever after.

Figure 4.5 A story used by D. Perry, Florence Primary School, Stoke-on-Trent, to initiate problem-solving activities

teacher could quite easily use the same challenges but encourage children to use various 'junk' materials in their constructions. Both approaches can be extremely successful in motivating the pupils and, as far as the science content is concerned, the ideas, the planning procedures, discussions and evaluations that pupils generate are the most important features of this exercise. This problem-solving approach can be followed up in more detail in Robert Johnsey's book, *Problem Solving in School Science*, as well as in the others listed at the end of the book.[3.]

And, finally, we come to the fourth point raised at the beginning of this chapter: the science that can arise spontaneously – which includes work that really presents too good an opportunity to miss and has got to have some space in the primary classroom.

Examples of these chance happenings are plentiful. In one school an investigation was initiated by a teacher who noticed that a new cloakroom floor became very slippery when pupils came in on a rainy day. Her class investigated different floor surfaces in an attempt to find out what properties made cloakroom floors safer and less slippery. I suspect that teachers will have no problem raising questions with pupils but may feel they need some support in helping pupils plan these investigations. Here, the various teacher resources published in the Science 5/13 series will prove to be the most invaluable resource.

Fortunately most primary schools can allow some flexibility in the planned work. These spontaneous questions are important to pursue sometimes – they might not make up a good sequence of science teaching but they do reinforce pupils' skills, make pupils aware of how useful scientific investigation can be, and keep links between science and the rest of the school curriculum. A judicious balance between pre-planned activities and incursion into the unexpected can, if adequate records are kept by each teacher, make a very lively and vibrant science programme for the year.

The case for a science coordinator

We must constantly remind ourselves of the great breadth of the primary curriculum that is in the main managed and taught by each teacher. Obviously this poses problems of expertise – few people can be an authority on all aspects of the pupils' daily diet and for that reason alone, if for no other, individuals within the school should be appointed to take on the special responsibility of developing a particular curriculum area. A special case must be made for science as it is still not being included in the curriculum of some schools and in others it has a marginal status. For those reasons and in order for science to get a place in primary school activities it seems essential to have someone in charge, someone to promote and champion its cause. My selection of the title 'science coordinator' is one that is, I feel, particularly appropriate for primary school organisation and, as the role of such a person is outlined, it will become clear that that title best fits the job description. The coordinating aspect of the work of the person in charge of science is paramount.

What exactly does a primary science coordinator do? Before we can describe the work of this person, we really have to outline the personal attributes that are necessary for that member of staff to promote science within the school. Primary schools do not have a tradition of conformity or uniformity – teachers are normally allowed, within certain limits, to teach as they please. Therefore, the idea of forcing staff to teach science or to stick rigidly to a syllabus is one that is anathema to the primary school teacher. The science coordinator's role can therefore only be fulfilled successfully if that person is liked and respected by the rest of the staff and is someone who can coerce or persuade colleagues without causing anxiety or acrimony. Sometimes appointments are made by headteachers who seem to forget the need for those attributes, with disastrous consequences. If the person concerned is one who gets on well with the staff and has some expertise to share, the job description then can and will vary in minor details according to the needs and resources of the school. I have included suggestions that have been accumulated from a variety of schools, infant and junior, and seem to me to represent the most useful aspects of a science coordinator's job. The list of duties might include:

- designing, through consultation, a syllabus that suits the other teachers. (Record-keeping comes into this and has been dealt with in part in chapter 3.)

75

- ensuring that a central core of reference material is available to all members of staff, knowing where to get hold of the books, workcards, etc. if they are not actually in the staffroom.
- storing and keeping track of apparatus/resources that are outside the normal class allocation, e.g., lenses, mirrors, stop clocks, plastic measuring cylinders, etc.
- attending in-service courses to collect new ideas and disseminating these to the rest of the staff through meetings or workshops
- teaching alongside reluctant or insecure colleagues in order to lessen their anxiety.

The second and third suggestions are ones that will be dealt with in chapter 5 and so need no further clarification here. There are, however, implications for the science coordinator in the implementation of the last two points. The science coordinator needs time away from normal classroom duties, for the success of the science programme will very largely depend on the amount of out-of-class time the headteacher is able to allocate to that individual for attending courses and helping colleagues develop their own confidence and expertise in science teaching.

One thing that has not been made explicit here is my feeling that science coordinators should not be responsible for teaching science to all the children in the school. That would dramatically alter the nature and place of science in the curriculum and would completely deny the possibility of any easy integration into other curriculum areas. The science coordinator would lose that all-essential role of coordinating colleagues, pupils, materials and syllabuses towards a worthwhile end: the teaching and learning of science. The aim should be for all the teachers in the school to tackle some science topics with their own classes and, if necessary, call upon the help and experience of the science coordinator. Keeping track of what pupils and staff do is an essential part of the job and simple checklists similar to ones described in previous chapters can be used.

Should a science coordinator be an expert in science? Should only graduate teachers with a considerable science input in their initial training be considered for the job? The answer is no, not necessarily. Obviously someone who has been educated so that they are familiar with sciences will be an asset, provided they also have the personal, social skills that have been emphasised. Also, many extremely successful science coordinators, particularly at the infant level, are people who have discovered an interest in science after they have been teaching for several years. They also make admirable science coordinators if they have the necessary communication skills. Such people have obviously had to spend more time acquiring the basic know-how to teach hitherto unfamiliar subject matter in perhaps a different way from teaching other aspects of the curriculum.

Science coordinators in the primary sector display a huge range of skills and areas of expertise and knowledge. The job of a science coordinator as delineated here is an onerous one but not one that excludes any particular individuals: the diverse nature of primary school teaching allows for an enormous variety of organisational strategies, and coordinators must fit into their own school situation. A science coordinator must be a sympathetic, well respected colleague with a great deal of tact, energy and enthusiasm. They must have a thirst for discovery and an even temperament. Given those attributes and an interest in science, almost anyone could qualify! In fact, those qualities are ones that are exhibited by the majority of primary school teachers – perhaps a difference of emphasis and direction is all that is needed here.

The Association for Science Education has produced a booklet entitled *Science and Primary Education Paper No. 3: A Post of Responsibility in Science*[4] which enumerates many of the points made above and is a good resource for schools. The usefulness of someone who can take charge of science and promote its cause sensitively amongst colleagues cannot be too highly acclaimed. The next chapter will deal with the less ideological decisions which have to be made concerning science, but which are no less of a problem for the science coordinator and the class teachers. Having decided when to teach science and what topics to choose, teachers must then turn to organising resources within the classroom so that the sheer amount of simple apparatus and the potential mess made are not deterrents to the pupils' engaging in science activities. In this way, decisions of principle and theory must always go hand in hand with practical considerations.

Classroom organisation

All school buildings are different: classrooms come in a variety of shapes and sizes, and it is impossible either to generalise about the provision of resources and amenities or to list the variety in existence. A useful way of ensuring that the classroom a teacher works in is conducive to doing science activities is to list the needs created by such activities and then ensure that it is possible, within the particular restraints imposed by the school, to match those needs as nearly as possible.

Classroom space and storage

The sort of primary science that has been described in previous chapters involves children in a large range of activities, some of which are messy. They may also be time-consuming or children may need space to work. Furthermore, storage space to leave items between experimental sessions may be necessary. All this has implications for the physical lay-out of the room and I have devised a series of questions which will help teachers to think about whether they are providing themselves with optimum conditions to encourage experimental work. The things that are essential to avoid are the situations in which practical science is not encouraged because either the lay-out of the room is not appropriate or any necessary equipment is not readily available.

Is the classroom organised so that pupils have a large enough surface area to work on?

Individual or paired desks are often not large enough and the necessity will occur, from time to time, to put desks together.

How easy is it for this to happen? Sometimes a variety of arrangements in the same room provide maximum flexibility – some individual desks, some grouped and perhaps a table. Again, this is an example of how important it is not to generalise about an individual classroom's provision, but science does sometimes need larger work surfaces than an individual desk will allow and somehow this requirement has to be provided. Teachers in classrooms with modern 'table-type' furniture will find this less difficult, but resourceful solutions have been found in situations where old, heavy desks are involved. One teacher's solution to the flat surface problem was to buy relatively cheap sheets of plywood which were not too heavy to handle, but which were strong enough to place on desks to make a flat surface, create surfaces by linking desks, or even to make into slopes or ramps when necessary.

Is your classroom organised in such a way as to encourage discussions to take place?

A space where pupils can go that is separated from their own desks if often a good idea. Infant classes often have a square of carpet where pupils can sit in a group round the teacher; some arrangement along the same lines would be useful in junior classrooms. A different atmosphere is produced when pupils physically move away from their desks and often a more fruitful discussion ensues as a result of this kind of regrouping. Discussions are a very important part of the science work of primary-aged pupils and it is essential to ensure that opportunities are provided for different-sized groups to make plans, discuss their possible experimental designs, and exchange information about the work that they have been doing.

Is there a shelf or cupboard where you can safely leave unfinished work?

There is always the problem of what to do with the inevitable half-made squeezy bottle clock, the robot with only one arm, or the collection of wood that a group will be testing for various properties. A setting-down place is remarkably important to the smooth running of the classroom. Bits and pieces that have been collected for further investigation can be moved from one place to another and become lost, damaged or separated, thus causing frustration and wasted time when they are needed again. Because of the investigative nature of primary science there is rarely a displayable end product but often a range of half-finished, partly tested designs. The inevitable question must arise: where am I going to get storage space in my small, overcrowded classroom? Somehow a place must be found, otherwise valuable time will be wasted. One suggestion might be to put up a shelf: one plank of contiboard (about 12" wide) fixed, if necessary, high up out of the way. It might not be very pleasing to look at but it will store a great deal of temporary experimental bits. Simple and obvious – but very useful.

Is equipment stored in such a way that all teachers have easy access to it?

The sort of apparatus and equipment that is needed specifically for scientific investigations may be more usefully stored centrally and managed by the science coordinator, but with each teacher having a store of 'essentials' within their own classroom. These two groups of materials may need different sorts of storage systems. The exact way in which items that are expensive and must therefore be shared are stored will vary according to the idiosyncrasies of school buildings and the predilections of the coordinator, but the following guidelines should be useful:

1 Resist the temptation to box equipment according to topics. Every teacher will approach the same theme in a different way. It is better to keep boxes of different materials – wood, plastics, metals – separate and allow teachers to select from them to suit their own activities.
2 Remember, even if you don't have much to store to start with, once science is an established part of the curriculum your collection will grow. Choose a storage spot that has the possibility for housing an expanding collection.
3 Aim for maximum accessibility for all members of staff. Colleagues will not feel inclined to hunt for the materials they need or browse through what is available if the storage space is in the coordinator's classroom. I have found that a

corner of the corridor near the science coordinator, who can give advice if necessary but need not be disturbed if it is inconvenient, is the most successful spot.

4 Devise a simple signing out system: one that can work very effectively is the 'slip' system. A small piece of paper is provided on which staff or pupils can write their names and what they have taken. They then drop these into a box. A periodic check on the box and a small reminder over coffee will usually retrieve the items, and at the same time a record can be kept of the use of consumable items.

5 If funds allow, a trolley with several drawers which is exclusively used for science work can be invaluable. With an arrangement like this, a teacher can borrow several whole collections from the central resource area and allow pupils to choose what they need as their experiments progress. In the examples in earlier chapters of work done on different materials, pupils (particularly the older ones) would have benefited from being encouraged to make choices and select the most appropriate items to test. It is often impractical to send individuals off to the resource bank, but it would be quite in order to allow them to hunt around in the boxes that have been brought to the classroom.

These guidelines are ones that have been distilled from a variety of successful arrangements and they present uncomplicated, workable solutions to the storage problem. The actual form of storage – whether in old shoe boxes, plastic trays or large boxes from the local supermarket – must remain up to individuals and as long as everything is clearly labelled, it doesn't seem to matter. Some further suggestions may be found in the ASE publication *Science and Primary Education Paper No. 3: A Post of Responsibility in Science.*[1]

Apparatus and materials

To include a suggested list of apparatus and other resources – apart from collections of materials, squeezy bottles and other assorted junk – can be counterproductive. You really don't need much specialist equipment but there are some items that I have found more use for than others. This is therefore not claiming to be an exhaustive list, but rather, a list of suggestions for starting your science resource bank:[2]

stop clocks
magnets
thermometers
mirrors
lenses
prisms
magnifying glasses
plastic measuring cylinders
batteries and small bulbs
wire (insulated)

All consumable items that are not exclusively used for science should ideally be stored in each classroom (and indeed are there already in most instances). Plasticine, yoghurt cartons, string, paper clips, and old newspapers are all examples of these and their presence in the classroom is no surprise to any primary school teacher as all these things are used in everyday classroom activities.

Much of the burden of amassing and organising a good collection of science resources falls upon the science coordinator. The great skill needed here is to make what is available easily accessible to all and to be good-humoured about minor breakages and mishaps. Obviously the better organised the collection of items is, the easier for all concerned, but in some ways organisational skills are not so much of a problem for the primary science coordinator as lack of funds to buy items that would increase the scope of the science teaching in the school. It is worth remembering that nearby secondary schools probably have what you need, and there are few heads of science who would refuse an approach by their feeder primary school. Indeed, many schools have established a system of borrowing equipment and using high school facilities. Yet another job for the overworked primary science coordinator?

6

Science outside the classroom

Throughout this book, attempts have been made to relate the science that pupils will be doing to their everyday experiences. Topics have been selected, as the examples in the text demonstrate, to give pupils some understanding of their environment and the world they live in through experimentation. Some may claim that this sort of aim falls within the domain of environmental studies programmes. Perhaps it does, too, but as has been illustrated repeatedly in this book, the boundaries of what constitutes science are and should be extremely blurred. This chapter will be concerned with the possibilities of doing science outside the classroom – by that I mean that the stimulus for exploration, the ideas for investigations, come from the child's experiences out of school. The home, parental workplaces, shops, parks and the countryside can all provide exciting stimuli for scientific projects or investigations. My intention is not to outline a whole project around these topics but to pick out a few scientific investigations which could easily arise from them. Just as in the discussions relating to the selection of content for science activities, the emphasis here will be on the way pupils carry out their investigations: the explorations and the scientific method will take precedence over the accumulation of facts.

The choice of topics is almost limitless and will vary from school to school depending on the locality and resources available. I have selected seven topics from which to extract some scientific investigations, and hope that these will serve as models or exemplars. Resource lists will be provided for each topic and, wherever possible, examples of how pupils have tackled similar projects. Much of the work suggested here will arise from pupils' visits to specific sites out of school and although the organisational and safety aspects of such activities are not included in the interests of brevity, their importance is not ignored – reference to those aspects will be made in the various resource lists.

Science at home

The home is perhaps the most appropriate starting point for science for most children. The kitchen is the one room in any house which provides many inspirations for investigations. Starting with food, Longman Scienceworld, *Science through Infant Topics B*, provides some interesting suggestions for teachers to initiate a study of milk (see Figure 6.1).

With older pupils, milk can form the basis of a study of preserving foods. By investigating different kinds of milk (e.g., pasteurised, sterilised, condensed, skimmed, untreated; and by varying the conditions under which it is stored, junior pupils can practise manipulating variables. Table 6.1 is designed to help teachers to sort out a plan of action:

Table 6.1 A table such as this one will enable pupils to manipulate variables

Type of Milk	Room Temp.	Very Cold (Fridge)	Warm (Boiler Room)	Hot (On Radiator)
Pasteurised				
Sterilised				
Condensed				
Skimmed				
Untreated				
Boiled Pasteurised				
Soya Milk				

Once again it would be unwise to present pupils with a ready-made table – the suggestions for types of milk and where to keep them should come from them. Once these have been decided upon, daily checks can be made of the samples and a date entered when each one shows signs of 'going off'. With older pupils it would be useful to speculate with them as to what made the milk go bad. You might lead them towards further experimentation by some questions like these:

Is there something in the milk that makes it go bad?
Is there something in the air that makes it go bad?
How can we design an experiment to find out whether something in the air makes the milk go bad?
Is there anything else that might make milk go off?
(Suggesting the possibility of dirty containers).

The ideas are similar in format to those suggested in previous chapters – discussions between pupils and teachers are of paramount importance and so are the opportunities for pupils to design their own experiments and perhaps make mistakes.

Eggs are a fascination to young children. Figure 6.2 is an example of some good work done by fourth-year juniors who tested the strength of different kinds of egg boxes. (This could also be extended to a much larger investigation including some craft and design work as pupils become involved with designing their own 'safe' egg boxes – see Figure 6.2.)

Further suggestions about experiments related to food and eating can be found in the following list, but a particularly useful publication is *Science in a Topic: Food*, in which there are suggestions for investigations of bread, sugar and salt.

Sources for 'food' topics

ASE, 'Dropping eggs', *Primary Science*, 6, autumn 1981.
ASE, 'Trials and errors with egg timers', *Primary Science*, 14, summer 1984.
ASE, 'Oranges and lemons', *Primary Science*, 16, spring 1985.
ASE, 'Changes in fairy cakes', *Primary Science*, 18, autumn 1985.
Bolton, D., 'Science Through Baking', *Primary Science Review*, 2, autumn 1986.

Language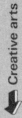

Mathematics

Physical education

Creative arts

Milk

Science

People and their jobs and occupations

Science activities

Starting points

Activities	Starter Book page	26
	Teachers' Book	86
M1 Drinking straw		86

Making and doing

Teachers' Book page 90

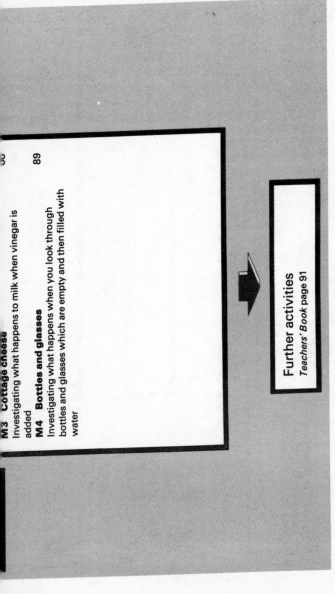

M3 Cottage cheese

Investigating what happens to milk when vinegar is added

M4 Bottles and glasses

Investigating what happens when you look through bottles and glasses which are empty and then filled with water

89

Further activities
Teachers' Book page 91

Figure 6.1 Investigating milk
(Source: Longman Scienceworld, *Science Through Infant Topics*, Teachers' Book B)

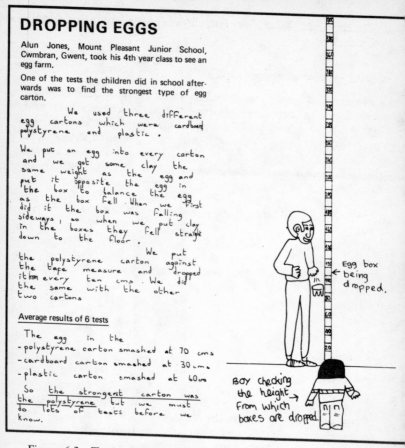

DROPPING EGGS

Alun Jones, Mount Pleasant Junior School, Cwmbran, Gwent, took his 4th year class to see an egg farm.

One of the tests the children did in school afterwards was to find the strongest type of egg carton.

We used three different egg cartons which were cardboard polystyrene and plastic.

We put an egg into every carton and we got some clay the same weight as the egg and put it opposite the egg in the box to balance the egg as the box fell. When we first did it the box was falling sideways, so when we put clay in the boxes they fell straight down to the floor.

We put the polystyrene carton against the tape measure and dropped it from every ten cms. We did the same with the other two cartons

Average results of 6 tests

The egg in the
- polystyrene carton smashed at 70 cms
- cardboard carton smashed at 30 cms
- plastic carton smashed at 60 cms

So the strongest carton was the polystyrene but we must do lots of tests before we know.

Egg box ← being dropped.

Boy checking the height → from which boxes are dropped.

Figure 6.2 Testing egg boxes
(Source: *Primary Science*, 6, autumn 1981)

Kincaid, D. and Coles, P., *Science in a Topic: Food*, Hulton Educational Ltd.

Longman Scienceworld: 'Milk', *Science Through Infant Topics, Book B*, p. 85.

'Theme: Food', *Junior Education*, February 1984.

Tooley, P., *Technology Around Us: Food and Technology*, Hart-Davis Educational Ltd.

West Sussex Science 5-14 Scheme, *Science Horizons Level 1*,

Cooking and What We Eat, West Sussex County Council, Chichester.

Sources for 'washing' topics

Examples of pupils' work published in *Primary Science* show the kind of activities associated with soap powders and washing. Studies of bubbles and comparisons between different strengths of soap solutions are two such investigations. Variables such as temperature of water and length of time cloth is soaked can be introduced as valuable for the children to study. Other suggestions can be found in the following:

ASE, 'Forever blowing bubbles', *Primary Science*, 10, spring 1983.
ASE, 'Which is the best soap powder?', *Primary Science*, 13, spring 1984.
ASE, 'Washing clothes and washing curtains', *Primary Science*, 14, summer 1984.
Longman Scienceworld, 'Jobs in the Kitchen', *Science Through Infant Topics*, Teacher Book B.

Sources for other 'home' topics

Other investigations arising from aspects of pupils' homes are topics considering various pieces of household machinery (telephones, egg-timers and simple electric circuits) and studies of the actual fabric of the house (materials used in its construction and problems associated with insulation). Some suggestions for suitable lines of investigation can be found in these resources:

Hayes, M. (ed), *Starting Primary Science*, 'Science from Everyday Things', Arnold.
Longman Scienceworld, 'Jobs in the Kitchen' *Science Through Infant Topics B*.
Science in a Topic: Communication.
Science in a Topic: Houses and Homes.

Shops and supermarkets

Even very young children are familiar with visits to shops and supermarkets but they may nonetheless be unaware of the possibilities for science that can arise from such an outing. Teachers can do much by taking pupils round a large supermarket; many store managers are willing to encourage a well-organised and orderly visit by a classful of primary-aged pupils. As not much experimentation – obviously – can take place *in situ* the teacher must help the pupils to observe carefully and encourage them to formulate the kinds of questions that can be followed up in school later. Numerous topics can arise, as this list indicates:

Fresh fruit and vegetables
– what parts of a plant are they?
Bread and cakes
– an exploration of the properties of yeast
Preservation
– drying: what happens when you add water to dried food?
– freezing: effect on different substances, investigation of ice and water
Sugar
– solubility in water
– harmful effects on teeth
Colours
– what is used to colour food?
– chromatography with Smarties, food colourings
Tins
– what are they made of?
– magnetic properties
– does the metal scratch?
Washing-up liquid
– which kind makes the biggest bubbles?
Soap powders
– which brand washes cleanest?
Carrier bags
– which supermarket provides the strongest bags?
– what happens to the bags when they get wet?

Trolleys
– how to make a smooth-running trolley
– friction
– ball-bearings
Cleaning materials
– which is the most effective on: different dirt, same surfaces/same dirt, different surfaces?
Flooring
– how slippery when wet?
Packaging
– why are things wrapped up?

Food preservation is one investigation I have selected to look at in greater detail. Here there is a confusion of variables for teacher and pupils to tease out. Pupils must identify different ways of food preservation:

freezing
canning
dehydrating
cooling
adding preservatives

They then investigate some of the properties of each method, perhaps in an attempt to explain why some are either more effective or more desirable than others. Some possibilities might be:

1 Freeze a variety of foods to see what happens when they are defrosted.
2 Add water to dehydrated foods and see how long they stay fresh. Examine the 'sell by' dates on the packets.
3 Try dehydrating fresh produce; weigh before and after to find the proportion of water.
4 Investigate cans: *Science in a Topic: Food* (p. 55) gives some useful suggestions involving testing for magnetic properties and scratching cans to see what the effect is.
5 Survey preservatives to see which are the most commonly used. Does a pattern emerge? Are some used for sweets and some for savouries? Do frozen foods have added preservatives?

Another useful investigation involves testing the products from a variety of supermarkets, particularly the bags provided to carry goods home. Here pupils can invent ways of testing materials for strength and waterproof properties, and relate these to size and function.

Sources for 'shops and supermarkets' topics

Longman Scienceworld, 'The shoeshop', 'The supermarket', 'The sweetshop', *Science Through Infant Topics B*.
Science in a Topic: Food, Hulton Educational.
'Theme: Food', *Junior Education*, February 1984.

Clothes and fabrics

Extending the range of investigations associated with pupils' home and school life might include some topics that children are particularly interested in, for example, the clothes they wear. A scientific study of these can be approached in a number of ways.

The study of different fabrics and their qualities can provide very fruitful investigations. Careful observations can be encouraged when pupils use hand-lenses or binocular microscopes to look at a variety of materials. Properties such as strength, elasticity, and waterproofing can be investigated by pupils designing their own experiments. All these properties of cloth and fabrics can be made particularly intriguing for pupils if they can be encouraged to bring scraps of material from home – that way they are finding out more about the clothes they have actually worn.

Keeping warm is a normal winter preoccupation and as a topic it can prompt a variety of investigations. 'What to do with the *Times Ed.*' in *Primary Science*, 10, spring 1983, gives an example of some work done by 7- and 8-year-olds. The children came to school with cold feet and this started them off investigating the insulating properties of newspapers.

Using dyes to change the colour of materials can be an interesting activity. Science can be introduced by

- varying the strength of manufactured dyes to see if it alters the final colour

- making dyes from nature, e.g., using extracts of red cabbage, beetroot, onion skins, blackberries and chopped-
- up grass
using different substances to fix the dyes to the cloth (mordants) and experimenting with the strength and quantities used.

Both boys and girls should be encouraged towards involvement in investigations associated with the clothes they wear. It is all too easy to pick on the girls' initial enthusiasm and allow boys to follow their interests into other areas of investigation, but we, as teachers, must be vigilant in our efforts to ensure that both boys and girls participate in all aspects of science. The investigations suggested here could be called the 'physics and chemistry of clothes' and range through all branches of science. A topic such as this one is an ideal vehicle to ensure equal participation of both boys and girls in science activities.

Sources for 'clothes and fabrics' topics

Bainbridge, J., *Man-made*, Evans.
'Project File: Clothes', *Child Education*, November 1985. (This includes an extensive booklist.)
Science in a Topic, Clothes and Costume, Hulton.
Teaching Primary Science Series: Fibres and Fabrics, Macdonald Educational.

Sports and games

Young children's enthusiasm for games and PE lessons can be an impetus to initiate some science. The list of possible activities is endless, so I have selected four activities which have proved good areas for investigation.

Balls are an obvious choice for both simple or more complicated studies. What starts off as a straight comparison of different kinds of balls and how high they bounce can produce some quite complicated design problems for the young scientist. How do you measure the height of bounce? How high off the ground does the ball have to be when you let it go? Those were only two of the problems that pupils encountered after starting what they thought was going to be a very straightforward piece of work. That led them to trying to bounce balls on different surfaces and, in the case of a squash ball, at different temperatures. All of these problems caused the pupils to think carefully about how they could eliminate variables and also how they could judge the accuracy of their findings.

The weekly visit to the swimming pool could initiate studies into streamlining, the use of flippers or paddles to increase speed, or even a comparison between sinking and floating objects. An enterprising teacher could even encourage some investigations at the pool-side – observations made during the swimming session will need further work or verification back at school.

Roller skating is a popular pastime which can provide opportunities for investigations. Careful questioning by the teacher can lead pupils to a study of friction (which surfaces are easier to roll on?) and a study of how to reduce friction using ball bearings (how can we make wheels run more smoothly?).

Children's activities in the playground can also cause enough interest to be followed up in lessons. *Primary Science*, 14, summer 1984, has an example of an autumn project: 'The strongest conkers'. The playground itself can also be used to good effect, as has been shown in the work of nursery and infant pupils in 'Making the most of a playground', *Primary Science*, 17, autumn 1985.

Sources for 'sports and games' topics

Gilbert, G. and Matthews, P., 'Bouncing balls', Card 71B, *Look: Primary Science*, Addison Wesley.
Gilbert, G. and Matthews, P., 'Sliding and Rolling', Card 67B, *Look: Primary Science*, Addison Wesley.
Science in a topic: Sports and Games.

Pets

Children are interested in animals and a class discussion about pets can usually be guaranteed to generate a great deal of interest. Many primary classrooms have gerbils, hamsters or fish which are lovingly cared for by pupils. Unfortunately, many of these creatures are kept in cramped, overcrowded and poorly ventilated conditions, and as a result of that their habits and life-styles do not easily suggest scientific investigations for pupils to undertake. I am not proposing that the animals should be experimented upon and thus risk being ill-treated in any way, but on the contrary, that a careful analysis of the animals' special needs, with particular reference to their housing requirements, may be the stimulus to scientific observations. Research in the school or public library will show pupils that most rodents – and gerbils in particular – are burrowing animals. Pupils can then devise interesting environments to allow their pets to burrow. A mixture of peat and straw in an old aquarium will allow gerbils to make a network of tunnels which will illustrate the animals' natural habitat. Pupils can provide a variety of materials for the animals to chew on – wooden blocks, old toilet roll holders and plastic guttering – to illustrate the effects of their powerful teeth. Apart from any science that we can extract from such activities, the main aim of the topic must be to educate children to care for their pets in a humane way and I suggest that the information gained from science can help them to do this.

Sources for 'pet' topics

Pets in the Eighties: A Teachers' Resource Pack, Pedigree Petfoods Education Centre, National Office, Waltham-on-the-Wolds, Melton Mowbray, Leics. LE14 4RS.

This contains an enormous amount of useful resource material and the Teachers' Handbook lists useful addresses.

RSPCA, (1985), *Animals in Schools*, RSPCA Education Dept.

Work and industry

Investigations that take pupils further away from their homes and domestic matters such as shopping might include a study of local industry. There is a great deal of interest in introducing children of junior age to the world of work, and industry in particular. HMI in their policy document *Science for All* suggest that:

The world of work

Alistair Ross outlines several different approaches to a project on industry

How can children begin to look at the world of work? They probably know quite a bit already: people are at work, or are looking for work, all around them. They've seen people working in shops and on the street. Many parents work – or at least would like to work. Schools are full of people working.

Junior schools can help focus and extend these experiences in three particular ways.

Visit a work-place

Visiting a work-place can be so much more than a day out. Find a local work-place that the children may know, and that is easy to get to on several occasions. Parents or school governors may help you to decide who to approach in a firm. A personal contact is best; otherwise write a short letter to the personnel manager and follow it up with a phone call.

Visit the work-place on your own first. Work out, with the firm, where the children will go and who they will be able to speak to. Try and arrange for them to meet as many different people as possible – supervisors, union officials, shop-floor workers and managers. Each will have a different perspective on what work is really like.

Find out, before the visit, who the children can speak to.

The first visit may not result in children asking all the questions you hope for – this will not happen until they have a mental image of the whole work-place. It's often on the second and third visit that children really begin probing with questions like these:

- Who tells you what to do?
- Can you tell anyone what to do?
- What happens if there's a disagreement about what to do?
- Is everyone paid the same?
- Why are there no women/men working here?
- Who decides what must be done?

Talking about the kinds of question to ask helps to focus ideas, but if the children write them down, this can lead to very stilted interviews. Instead, either tape-record them or make notes yourself. A photo of each person you speak to, and their name, can help classroom discussion enormously (it's so much easier to refer to 'Pete' than 'the big man with red hair behind the counter').

Back in school, get children to make models of what happens – perhaps to show how the work-place is organised, rather than how it looks. Discuss and make charts of the organisation of the work-place, or a mobile to show who's in charge.

Experiment with the processes the children have seen. Start a role-playing drama about the place they have visited – *what would happen if a machine broke down, or the orders weren't coming through?* Above all, discuss the experiences. Bring some of the people you met at the work-place into school to show them what you've been doing, and to give the children a chance to talk with them further.

Mini-enterprises

Starting a mini-enterprise means that children will have to make their own product, or provide a service, for real. Children have made and sold mugs, cakes or magazines, have run the school tuck shop, and so on.

Before they start, they need to decide what customers want, and find the money to start off their industry. *Will they be a co-operative financed by themselves equally, or ask for a loan from the school, or visit the local bank?*

They must then decide how to organise themselves and run a production line. *How will they market and sell themselves, and how will they keep accounts?* A few enterprising infant classes have done all this, so there's no excuse for juniors! The range of work coming out of this can be enormous.

Simulations

Simulating an industry isn't doing it for real in the same way. For example, a class could make something – cakes, or Christmas decorations – in different ways. Perhaps some could work on a production line, and some individually. Afterwards they talk about what they've done. *Who made the most? Which look all the same? Who enjoyed themselves most?*

A classroom shop can be much more than an exercise in using money. *What do the shops do with stock they can't sell? What about extra supplies of fast-moving lines? What overheads will they have to pay, and how much will the shop workers wages be?*

Figure 6.3 Initiating topic work on industry
(Source: Topic pack 'The world of work', *Junior Education*, June 1986)

> In reviewing policies for, and practice in, science education for pupils throughout the compulsory age range, the Secretaries of State believe that LEAs, schools, teachers, parents, examination boards, employers...may find it helpful to analyse what is provided in terms of the following: ...Relevance: science education should draw extensively on the everyday experience of pupils, and should be aimed at preparing pupils as effectively as possible for adult and working life...

The June 1986 edition of *Junior Education* includes a topic pack on industry and in Figure 6.3, which is an extract from the pack, there is a summary of how teachers can set about initiating and carrying out work associated with industry.

After an introductory visit such as the one described in Figure 6.3, how is it possible to get some investigative science from the pupils' observations? To get maximum benefit from any visit and for good follow-up work to emerge, the teacher and the contact person have to liaise very carefully and it is helpful if they can actually pre-arrange some explanations and questions which the teacher can ensure will lead to further work. An example of this is given in this description of a visit by a class of eight-year-olds to a pottery factory where they make tableware of various sorts which is decorated both by handpainting and applying stencils.

The teacher and the guide discussed with the class the medium the potters use to make the cups and saucers – words like 'clay', 'slip', and 'bone china' were introduced to the children and they were allowed to handle all the raw materials. They were told that clay came from the ground but that it had been brought from another part of the country where there was good clay for making pots. The children watched plates being painted and discussed with the painters what sort of paints they used. It was impressed upon the children how important it was to ensure that the decorations did not come off the plates when they were washed. The pupils saw the kilns and were told how hot they had to be to fire the crockery. When they returned to school with a bag of clay, a box of samples and some broken bits of pottery, their teacher, in the course of the follow-up discussion, started to generate 'I wonder if...?' questions.

I wonder if we could use earth from near here to make plates?
I wonder if there is clay in our local soil?
I wonder what clay soil looks like?
I wonder what different kinds of soils we can find?
I wonder if we could paint a waterproof design on some old plates? What sort of paints are waterproof?
I wonder how hot the school oven is? I wonder if that is hot enough to fire our clay? (Beware of using an oven that is used in food preparation – the clay objects you make may explode and damage the oven if you leave any air bubbles in the clay.)

That is one way of extending and utilising a visit to a factory. The 'Industry' topic pack has some further suggestions and contains a good bibliography including these useful addresses for obtaining resources and information:

School Curriculum Industries Project, Newcombe House, 45 Notting Hill Gate, London W11 3JB.
Science and Technology Regional Organisation, SCSST, 1 Birdcage Walk, London SW1H 9JJ.
Understanding British Industry Resource Centre, Sun Alliance House, New Inn Hall Street, Oxford, OX1 2QE.

These organisations will supply resources and information of a general nature, but for maximum impact on pupils a local factory or workshop should be selected – perhaps one in which some of the children's parents work. This would have the additional advantage of encouraging links between the school and parents, and provides an opportunity of including parents in some aspects of their children's work.

Sources for 'work and industry' topics

Jamieson, Ian, *We Make Kettles: Studying Industry in the Primary School*, Longman for SCDC Publications.
'Project file: industry', *Child Education*, February 1987. This gives further examples of pupil's work arising from visits to a fruit-pie factory, a pottery and a paint (pigment) manufacturer.

Environment and field studies

The area of field studies really warrants a separate book of its own and no real justice can be done to it in the few pages allocated here. However, no discussion of science outside the school would be complete without mention of the value of in-depth studies of different natural environments. The book list provided will give interested teachers some useful starting points for planning schemes of work with worthwhile scientific content. All I will attempt to do in this chapter is to lay down a few guidelines to help teachers to ensure that whatever their chosen arena for study (this could include parks, recreation areas, open countryside, common land, ponds, rivers, streams, farmland or field study centres) some science is being taught. It is all too easy to make a visit to a park or a playing field and omit any scientific investigations. Surveys quantifying the plants and animals have only a limited use for pupils and any studies should ideally concentrate on relating quantity to environmental conditions. For example, a study of the worn patches of grass in a park should include a survey of the use people make of the park as well as a mapping of any large objects such as trees and buildings. Explanations can begin to be formulated as to why the grass is not growing at a uniform rate and these speculations can be followed up at school by further experiments. If three areas of grass are marked off and subjected to different treatment - walking daily on one bit, mowing another regularly and allowing the other to grow freely – some further understanding about the nature of grass as a living organism may be arrived at. Observations should lead to questions, and in the answering of the questions children should be encouraged to follow the same sort of scientific processes that have been advocated throughout this book.

Sources for 'environment and field study' topics

Some good ideas that will help teachers design work that will enable their pupils to explore their environment can be found in the following publications.

ASE, 'Our school field', *Primary Science*, summer 1983.

ASE, 'Ponds', *Primary Science*, autumn 1984.

Cheshire County Council (1985), *Outdoor Education Guidelines*, Eaton Press.

Clark, A. Pollock, S. and Wells, P., *Links*: project pack in ecology for 9-13 year-olds, Cambridge Educational.

Jennings, T. J. (1971), *Collecting from Nature*, Wheaton.

Jennings, T. J. (1985), *The Young Scientist Investigates: Pond Life*, Oxford University Press.

McArthur, J., Graham, I. and Macaskill, M. (1985), *Starting Points: In the Park*, Hulton Educational Publications Ltd.

Nicholls, A. (1971), *On the Road*, Ginn & Co. Ltd.

Nuffield Junior Science (1967), *Teachers' Guide 2*, Collins.

Science 5/13, *Early Investigations, Investigations* 1 and 2,

Tackling Problems 1 and 2, *Ways and Means, Using the Environment*; *Trees*, Stages 1 and 2, Macdonald Educational.

Stannard, P. (1976), *Man and Nature: Animals, Plants and Places*, Macmillan Education.

'Topic file: trees', *Junior Education*, March 1984.

Conclusion

These suggestions for science topics that can emerge from stimuli outside the classroom are included in order to widen the range and scope of activities. However, the message remains constant throughout this book – it's the *way* the science is tackled that is important, not any specific *content*. But, having said that, both teachers and pupils will benefit from a variety of investigations and those stimulated by or instigated only in pupils' classrooms are just a small portion of what is available. Looking outside the school can bring a different dimension to science teaching and learning.

References

Chapter 1 Primary science in perspective

1 W. Harlen, *Science at Age 11: APU Science Report for Teachers*, London, HMSO, 1980.
2 Report of the Central Advisory Council for Education (England), *Children and their Primary Schools* (The Plowden Report), London, HMSO, 1967.
3 Science 5/13 Series, *Teachers' Guides* (26 Titles), London, Macdonald Educational, 1972-5.
4 Nuffield Junior Science, *Teachers' Guides 1 & 2*, London, Collins Educational, 1967.
5 Department of Education and Science, *Primary Education in England: A Survey by HM Inspectors of Schools*, London, HMSO, 1978.
6 Department of Education and Science, *Science 5 – 16: A Statement of Policy*, London, HMSO, 1985.

Chapter 2 The framework for planning science activities

1 B. Hodgson and E. Scanlon, (eds), *Approaching Primary Science*, New York, Harper & Row, 1985. This book contains a selection of articles, and 'What is science?', by the United Nations Educational, Scientific and Cultural Organisation, is the one quoted in this chapter.
2 C. Gilbert and P. Matthews, *Primary Science*, London, Addison-Wesley, 1981.
3 This topic on streamlining was prepared by the class teacher using a variety of resources, including:
ASE, *Primary Science*, 12, autumn 1983.

J. Bryant, *Shipshape, Level 2b, Science Horizons*, Chichester, West Sussex County Council, 1982.

Science 5/13, 'Boats', Section 6 *Science from Toys*, London, Macdonald Educational, 1972-5.

4 ASE, *Primary Science*, 12, autumn 1983. The whole issue deals with the topic 'movement', and the work on toy parachutes is an example of work done by some junior pupils. There are also some interesting examples of infant work included in the same issue.

5 P. Black, 'Science, technology and the primary school child,' a lecture given at the Standing Conference on Schools' Science and Technology, 14 November 1984.

6 Useful resources dealing with technology in the classroom include:

'Implementation of guidelines, flowcharts, 5 – 13 years', *CDT: Statement of Objectives*, Stafford, Staffordshire County Council, 1985.

R. Johnsey, *Problem Solving in School Science*, London, Macdonald Educational, 1986.

Science and Technology in the Primary School, Standing Conference on Schools Science and Technology, 14 November 1984.

P. Williams and D. Jinks, *Design and Technology*, London, Falmer Press, 1985.

7 Hodgson and Scanlon, op. cit. Part three deals particularly with pupil's intellectual growth.

8 W. Harlen, (ed.), *Primary Science: Taking the Plunge*, London, Heinemann, 1985.

9 Other useful resources include:

H. M. E. Barber and J. T. Hayes, *Exploring the Physical World with Children of 5 to 9*, London, J. M. Dent & Sons Ltd, 1973.

D. Diamond, *Introduction and Guide to Teaching Primary Science*, London, Macdonald Educational, 1978. (This introductory guide is linked to a series of useful resource books including volumes entitled: *Candles, Seeds and Seedlings, Science from Waterplay, Fibres and Fabrics, Mirrors and Magnifiers, Musical Instruments*.)

M. Hayes, *Starting Primary Science*, London, Edward Arnold, 1982. B. L. Young, *Teaching Primary Science*, Harlow, Longman, 1979.

All these publications are in addition to those already listed and those specifically used in connection with topics developed in subsequent chapters.

Chapter 3   Planning what to teach: content choice

1   W. Harlen, *Science at Age 11: APU Science Report for Teachers*, London, HMSO, 1980.

2   D. Kincaid and P. Coles, *Houses and Homes, Science in a Topic*, Amersham, Hulton Educational Publications Ltd, 1981.

3   A selection of resources for science work in insulating materials could include:

ASE, *Burning, Warmth and Sunlight* (Book 2), *Experiencing Energy*, ASE 1980. (See chapter 8, 'Getting warm and keeping warm'.)

ASE, *Primary Science*, 16, spring 1985 – particularly the work on cavity walls.

Schools Council, *Materials, Learning Through Science*, London, Macdonald Educational, 1985. (This unit contains a collection of 24 pupils' work cards and a teacher's booklet providing useful ideas for all the four class topics considered in this chapter. The pupil cards 'Teapots' and 'Cups, Mugs and Beakers' contributed activities for the first-year teacher to incorporate into her plans.)

West Sussex Science 5-14 Scheme (Hobbs, Hudson, Moreland and Slack), Level 2a, *Keeping Our Home Warm*, *Science Horizons*, London, Macmillan Educational, 1981-2.

4   Resources for the study of the properties of bricks and building materials include:

J. W. Bainbridge, R. W. Stockdale and E.R. Wastnedge, *Junior Science Source Book*, London, Collins, 1970.

Kincaid and Coles, op. cit., section 3, 'Walls'.

J. McArthur, I. Graham and M. Macaskill *Our Homes; Starting Points*, Amersham, Hulton Educational Publications Ltd, 1985.

'Project file: houses and homes', *Child Education*, January 1984.

5   Resources used include the following:
    Insight to Science – *Materials* – various pupils cards, Addison Wesley.
    Learning through Science, *Materials*. Pupils work card, 'Tools'.
    Science 5/13, *Trees*, Stages 1 and 2, Macdonald Educational.
    Science 5/13, *Working with Wood*, Stages 1 and 2.
    Science 5/13, *Working with Wood*, Background.

6   Resources used include the following:
    Insight to Science, *Materials* and *Air and Heat*, Addison Wesley. (These two units consist of a series of pupil work cards and a teacher's guide for each one. They were written specifically for 11 – 13 year olds but there are good ideas on the cards for teachers to adapt.)
    D. Kincaid and P. Coles, *Science in a Topic: Houses and Homes* and *Ships*, Amersham, Hulton Educational Publishers, 1981.
    Science 5/13, *Change*, Stages 1 and 2, Macdonald Educational.
    Science 5/13, *Metals*, Background.
    Science 5/13, *Metals*, Stages 1 and 2.

7   Blocks of comparable-sized materials – woods, metals, glass, polystyrene and other – can be obtained from: Solid Materials Kit, Griffin & George Ltd, Bishop Meadow Road, Loughborough, Leics. LE11 0RG.

8   County of Avon, *Primary Science, A Policy for Science* (Guidelines for science in the primary school), Avon Education Committee. Cheshire County Council, *Primary Science Guidelines*.

9   A. Ward, *A Source Book for Primary Science*, London, Hodder & Stoughton, 1983.

Chapter 4   The organisation of science within the primary curriculum

1   H. Bradley, J. Eggleston, T. Keny and D. Cooper, *Developing Pupils' Thinking Through Topic Work: A Starter Course*, Harlow, Longman, 1985.

2   All the books and schemes of work suggested here suggest a large variety of topics which can be loosely grouped together as biological investigations; this is by no means an exhaustive list – just a selection of useful items:

O. N. Bishop, *Outdoor Biology*, London, John Murray, 1971. (This is a series of three books and a teacher's guide, none of which are really suitable for direct use by pupils, but they are all admirable resources for teachers.)

O. N. Bishop, *Adventures with Small Plants*, London, John Murray, 1983.

I. Finch, *Nature Study and Science*, Harlow, Longman, 1985.

Learning Through Science is a project jointly sponsored by the Schools Council and the Scottish Education Department, consisting of a series of units containing cards for children and notes for teachers (much of the work is based on the *Science 5/13* material) – the most applicable units are *Out of Doors, All Around* and *Which and What*.

Science 5/13, *Early Explorations, Investigations 1 & 2, Tackling Problems 1 & 2, Ways and Means*, in *Using the Environment* (series), London, Macdonald Educational, 1974.

E. Soothill and M. J. Thomas, *Nature Trek in Spring*, Littleborough, Naturetrek Educational Books, 1983.

T. Trevor and M. Linton, *Outside Now*, London, Bell & Hyman Ltd – this consists of a series of booklets suggesting outdoor activities appropriate for different months of the year (each booklet covers two months, *January and February* being the first volume).

3   Other useful resources dealing with problem-solving:

BBC Education Television, *Investigating Science – Teachers' Notes*, London, BBC Enterprises Ltd, 1986.

British Association for the Advancement of Science, *Ideas for Egg Races*, 1983.

R. Johnsey, *Problem Solving in School Science*, London, Macdonald Educational, 1986.

D. Shaw, 'Practical Problem-solving', *Junior Education*, June 1986.

P. Williams and D. Jinks, *Design and Technology 5-12*,

London, Falmer Press, 1985.
4   ASE, 'A post of responsibility in science' *Science and Primary Education Papers No. 3*: Hatfield, Association for Science Education, 1981.

Chapter 5   Classroom organisation

1   Examples of various ways of storing equipment can be found in:
ASE (1981), 'A post of responsibility in science' *Science and Primary Education Paper No. 3*, Hatfield, Association for Science Education, 1981.
Nuffield Junior Science, *Teacher's Guide 1*, London, Collins Educational, 1970. Science 5/13.
With Objectives in Mind, London, Macdonald Educational, 1972.
2   Further suggestions for useful equipment for teaching primary science are given in:
ASE, 'A post of responsibility in science'.
J. W. Bainbridge, R. W. Stockdale and E. R. Wastnedge, *Junior Science Resource Book*, London, Collins, 1970.
C. Gilbert and P. Matthews, *Look: Primary Science*, Teachers' Guides A and B, Wokingham, Addison Wesley, 1981.
Learning Through Science, *Science Resources for Primary and Middle Schools*, London, Macdonald Educational, 1980.
Nuffield Junior Science (1967), *Teachers' Guides 1 and 2*, London, Collins Educational, 1967.
West Sussex County Council, *Science Horizons, Teachers' Handbook*, London, Macmillan Educational, 1981.

Bibliography

Aitken, J. and Mills, J., 1982, *Infant Science Masters* and *Primary Science Masters*, Holmes McDougall, Edinburgh.

ASE, 1980-1985, *Primary Science*: 1-18, Association for Science Education, Hatfield.

ASE, 1985, *Choosing Published Primary Science Materials for Use in the Classroom*, Association for Science Education, Hatfield.

ASE, 1980, *Moving Things, Experiencing Energy* (Book 1): A Source Book for Teachers in Primary and Middle Schools, Association for Science Education, Hatfield.

ASE, 1980, *Burning, Warmth and Sunlight, Experiencing Energy* (Book 2). A Source Book for Teachers in Primary and Middle Schools, Association for Science Education, Hatfield.

ASE, 1981, *The Headteacher and Primary Science, Science and Primary Education Papers* 2, Association for Science Education, Hatfield.

ASE, 1981, *A Post of Responsibility in Science, Science and Primary Education Paper 3*, Association for Science Education, Hatfield.

ASE, 1980, *Language in Science*, Study Series 16, Association for Science Education, Hatfield.

Avon County Council, 1982, *A Policy for Science: Guidelines for Science in the Primary School*, Avon County Council, Bristol.

Bailey, A. and Wilcox, H., 1987, *Longman Scienceworld: Junior Teacher Books 1 and 2* and *Junior Pupils' Books 1 and 2*, Longman, Harlow.

Bainbridge, J. W., Stockdale, R. W. and Wastnedge, E. R., 1970, *Junior Science Source Book*, Collins, London.

Barber, H. M. E. and Hayes, J. T., 1973, *Exploring the Physical World with Children of 5 to 9*, J. M. Dent and Sons Ltd, London.

Barker Lunn, J., 1984, 'Junior school teachers: their methods and practices', *Educational Research*, 26, 3.

Bellett, D. J., 1985, 'Primary education, science and technology: A different PEST in the classroom', *Education in Science*, 111, January 1985.

Bird, J. and Diamond, D., 1975, *Teaching Primary Science*: *Candles*, Macdonald Educational, London.

Bishop, O. N., 1971, *Outdoor Biology*, John Murray, London.

Bishop, O. N., 1983, *Adventures with Small Plants*, John Murray, London.

Black, P., 1984, 'Science, technology and the primary child', a lecture given at the Standing Conference on Schools' Science and Technology, 14 November 1984.

Bradley, H., Eggleston, J., Keny, T. and Cooper, D., 1985, *Developing Pupils' Thinking Through Topic Work: A Starter Course*, Longman, Harlow.

Briggs, F., 1976, *Starting Science*, Macmillan Education, London.

Bright Ideas, 1984, *Science*, Scholastic Publications Ltd, Leamington Spa.

British Association for the Advancement of Science, 1983, *Ideas for Egg Races*.

Brophy, M., 1985, 'Primary science: some contradictions', *School Science Review*, 66, 236.

Central Advisory Council for Education, 1967, *Children and their Primary Schools* (The Plowden Report), HMSO, London.

Cheshire Education Department, 1982, *Primary Science Guidelines*, Cheshire County Council.

Cheshire County Council, 1985, *Outdoor Education Guidelines*, Eaton Press Ltd, Chichester.

Child, C. 1987, 'Problem-solving: science or technology?', *Primary Science Review*, 4, summer 1987.

Child Education Project Files: 'Houses and Homes', January 1984; 'Science', July 1985; 'Clothes', November 1985; 'Towns and Cities', September 1986; 'Farm Animals', January 1987; 'Industry', February 1987.

Clark, A., Pollock, S. and Wells, P., *Links*: Project pack in ecology for 9-13 year olds, Cambridge Educational.

DES, 1978, *Primary Education in England: A Survey by HM Inspectors of Schools*, HMSO, London.

DES, 1983, *Science in Schools: Age 11*, Report 2, HMSO, London.

DES, 1985, *Science 5-16: A Statement of Policy*, HMSO, London.

DES/HM Inspectors of Schools, 1985, *The Curriculum − from 5-16*, HMSO, London.

Diamond, D., 1976, *Mirrors and Magnifiers, Teaching Primary Science*, Macdonald Educational, London.

Diamond, D., 1978, *Introduction and Guide to Teaching Primary Science*, Macdonald Educational, London.

Edwards, R. *et al.*, 1982, *Exploring Primary Science: A Teachers' Handbook* and *Pupil Materials*, Cambridge University Press, Cambridge.

Finch, I., 1971, *Nature Study and Science*, Longman, Harlow.

Bibliography

Gilbert, C. and Matthews, P., 1981, *A First Look*, *Look A* and *Look B*, Addison-Wesley, London.

Hargrave, E. and Brooks, J., 1986, *Longman Scienceworld: Science through Infant Topics*, Longman, Harlow.

Harlen, W., 1978, 'Does content matter in primary schools?', *School Science Review*, 59.

Harlen, W., 1980, *Science at Age 11: APU Science Report for Teachers*, HMSO.

Harlen, W. (Ed.), 1985, *Primary Science: Taking the Plunge*, Heinemann, London.

Hayes, M., 1982, *Starting Primary Science*, Edward Arnold, London.

Hodgson, B. and Scanlon, E., 1985, *Approaching Primary Science*, Harper & Row, New York.

Jamieson, I., 1984, *We Make Kettles: Studying Industry in the Primary School*, Longman for SCDC Publications, London.

Jennings, J. J., 1985, *The Young Scientist Investigates: Pond Life*, Oxford University Press, Oxford.

Johnsey, R., 1986, *Problem Solving in School Science*, Macdonald Educational, London.

Junior Education, 'Theme: Food', February 1984 and 'Theme: Trees', March 1984.

Kincaid, D. and Coles, P., 1981, *Science in a Topic* (various titles), Hulton Educational Publications Ltd, Amersham.

Learning through Science Project, 1980, *Science Resources for Primary and Middle Schools*, Macdonald Educational, London.

Learning through Science Project, 1980, *Science for Children with Learning Difficulties*, Macdonald Educational, London.

Learning through Science Project, 1980 onwards, various titles, Macdonald Educational, London.

Leyland, P., 1985, 'Teaching the teachers', *Education in Science*, 112, April 1985.

McArthur, J., Graham, I. and Macaskill, M., 1985, *Starting Points: In the Park*, Hulton Educational Ltd, Amersham.

Matthews, P., 1984, 'Processed Pooh' School Science Review, 66, 235, December 1984.

Mills, G., 1981, *Science Skills*, Collins Educational, London.

Murray, E. and Crittenden, R. (1986), *Science Scene Setters*, published for British Gas by Collier Searle Matfield Ltd.

Nicholls, A., 1971, *On the Road*, Ginn & Co. Ltd, Aylesbury.

Nuffield Combined Science, 1980, *Themes for the Middle Years* (various titles), Longman, Harlow.

Nuffield Junior Science, 1967, *Animals and Plants, Apparatus, Teachers' Guides 1 and 2*, Collins Educational, London.

Open University, 1986, *EHP531 Primary Science*, Open University Press, Milton Keynes.

Perkins (ed.), 1962, *The Place of Science in Primary Schools*, The British Association.

Pets in the Eighties: A Teachers' Resource Pack, Pedigree Petfoods Education Centre.

Pollock, S., 1986, 'Making a museum visit work for you', *Primary Science Review*, 2, autumn 1986.

Redman, S., Brereton, A. and Boyers, P., 1969, *An Approach to Primary Science*, Macmillan, London.

Richards, C., Holford, D, (eds.), 1983, *The Teaching of Primary Science: Policy and Practice*, Falmer Press, London and New York.

Richards, R., 1980, 'Children's learning through science', *Education 3-13*, 8, 2.

R.S.P.C.A., 1985, *Animals in Schools*, R.S.P.C.A. Education Department.

Science 5/13, 1974, *Early Explorations, Investigations 1 and 2, Tackling Problems 1 and 2, Ways and Means in Using the Environment* (series), Macdonald Educational, London.

Science 5/13, 1972, *With Objectives in Mind*, Macdonald Educational, London.

Science 5/13, 1972-1975, *Teachers' Guides* (26 titles), Macdonald Educational, London.

Shaw, D., 'Practical Problem-solving', *Junior Education*, June 1986.

Showell, R., 1983, *Practical Primary Science: A Source Book for Teachers*, Ward Lock Educational, London.

Showell, R., 1979, *Teaching Science to Infants*, Ward Lock Educational, London.

Soothill, E. and Thomas, M. J., 1983, *Nature Trek in Spring*, Naturetrek Educational Books, Littleborough.

Staffordshire Education Authority, 1985, *CDT: Statement of Objectives, Implementation of Guidelines, Flowcharts, 5-13 Years*, Staffordshire County Council, Stafford.

Stannard, P., 1966, *Man and Nature: Animals, Plants & Places*, Macmillan Education, London.

Titley, F., 1987, 'Can we show you round the trail?', *Primary Science Review*, 4, summer 1987.

Tooley, P., 1977, *Technology Around Us: Food and Technology*, Hart-Davis Educational Ltd, London.

Trevor, T. and Linton, M., 1985, *Outside Now*, Bell & Hyman, London.

Tunnicliffe, S. and Wisely, C., 1987, 'Richmond Primary Technology Unit', *Education in Science*, 122, April 1987.

Ward, A., 1983, *A Source Book for Primary Science Education*, Hodder & Stoughton, London.

Ward, A., 1984, 'Science in an integrated primary school project on water – an inspiration', *School Science Review*, 66, 235, December 1984.

Ward, A., 1980, 'Thoughts on the style of primary science', *School Science Review*, 61, 216, March 1980.

West Sussex County Council, 1981, *Science Horizons, Teachers' Handbook*, Macmillan Education Ltd, Basingstoke.

West Sussex Science Scheme (Hobbs, Hudson, Moreland & Slack), 1982, *Science Horizons: Keeping our Home Warm*, Level 2a, Macmillan Education, London.

West Sussex 5-14 Scheme, 1985, *Science Horizons*, Macmillan Education, London. (Various topics in levels 2a and 2b and Teacher's Handbook.)

Williams, P. and Jinks, D., 1985, *Design and Technology 5-12*, Falmer Press, London and New York.

Wood, D., 1987, 'The metamorphosis of a primary science teacher', *Primary Science Review*, 4, summer 1987.

Young, B. L., 1979, *Teaching Primary Science*, Longman, Harlow.

Young Scientist Investigates, (various titles), Oxford University Press.

Index